About the covers:

Front cover: Photograph taken by Deb Wood on the morning
Joey crossed over the Rainbow Bridge.

Deb: "What a glorious sight to see as Heaven received our precious Joey."

Back cover: Taken by Deb Wood

Cover designs by PENtagram Consulting

Joey's Morning
The Legacy of a Therapy Horse
Copyright 2013 by Mary Ann Hutchison

JOEY'S MORNING

The Legacy of a Therapy Horse

BY

Mary Ann Hutchison

With

Deb Wood

DEDICATION

To my husband and soul mate, Bill, who designed and built our Wood Haven facility, a wonderful healing center of peace and refuge for all who enter. And,

To Sir Joey, for opening the pathway to emotional healing for himself and everyone in his presence.

--- Deb Wood

ABOUT THE AUTHOR

Mary Ann Hutchison calls Tucson, Arizona home. Her immediate family begins with one husband, two spoiled felines, six children, twenty grandchildren, and eight great-grandchildren.

Her writing family derives from the Arizona Mystery Writers, where she's the current Speaker Chair and past Presiding Chair.

She's a Past Member of the Society of Southwestern Authors and the Society of Children's Book Writers and Illustrators.

She's one of five Tucson writers who call themselves "Gecko Gals Ink," and are described as "sassy and spunky authors who write in a variety of genres and conduct writing workshops and seminars."

In addition to three novels, her short stories and memoirs are included in *Gecko Tales, Good Old Days* magazine, *Thanksgiving to Christmas: A Patchwork of Stories, A Way With Murder Anthology,* and *Take Me Out to the Love Game,* co-written with Carol Costa, which contains the true story of how she stalked John Wayne, found him, and wound up in his arms.

ACKNOWLEDGEMENTS

Many hands, hearts and hooves went into the telling of *Joey's Morning*. In addition to the contributors, I want to thank Victoria (Tori) Weatherly, my granddaughter, and Nancy Hall, my friend of sixty-three years, who labored as editors; Ashleen O'Gaea(a Gecko Gal) who brought me out of the maze I was lost in while writing the book, taught me how to work with Create Space, *and* designed the covers from photos by Deb Wood; my Gecko Gals Carol Costa, Dewanne Tremont and Jude Johnson, who supported me when I faltered; my family who have always encouraged me in everything I've ever done; *all* of the horses, my wonderful horses, who taught me how to live the rest of my life. And, as always, my husband, Doug, who drives me everywhere, listens to me rant, does most of the cooking, and spends hours alone while I'm in writing mode. I love you all.   Mary Ann Hutchison

ABOUT DEB WOOD

The Collaborator of Joey's *Morning,* lives on three acres in Marana, Arizona, with her husband, Bill, their six horses and three Dalmatians. They call it their "little slice of Heaven, where people and animals alike find peace and serenity."

Deb's true passion is to help others understand the importance of healing the emotional body which will in turn heal the physical and Spiritual bodies. She's chosen to do this by way of the horse.

OTHER BOOKS
BY MARY ANN HUTCHISON

MOOCHI'S MARIACHIS:

The joys and angst of teens hasn't changed in centuries; no matter the era or location, basically, they're the same. Share the early teen years of Moochi, Chico, Ladybug and Turo as their friendship is tested, then shaken by unforeseen problems. The answers may lie in the surrounding desert which, in turn, offers them safe haven as well as danger.

RAIN, RAIN, GO AWAY…:

Eight-year old Betsy Ann is in trouble: she wants her dolly to die; she draws pictures of gravestones. Meanwhile, the Judge and Staff of Division Three, San Ramon County Superior Court, prepare to sentence the Santa Klaus Killer. To those who labor in the judiciary and law enforcement, two things are well-known: time is of the essence; there's one thing in knowing, another in the proving. It's implicit that no matter their vocation, what they do after hours must be something that will shatter the images of what they consistently see and hear.

CASCABEL — Treachery's Reward:

The wide open Western Frontier in 1865 paints the backdrop for murder and revenge. A young man's manic need to avenge the deaths of his family is aided by an Apache woman warrior. Skilled in the art of war and killing, she becomes his teacher and lover. A man's mind can become ingenious when he begins sinking into insanity. Filled with venom, he becomes *"El Cascabel"* (Spanish for rattlesnake).

PROLOGUE

I met Deb Wood in December 2011 at a Business Women's Luncheon in Tucson, Arizona. As tablemates, we chatted in that "getting-to-know-another" way, and soon, the conversation turned to her beloved Sir Joey, who'd trotted over the Rainbow Bridge in January of that year.

She casually mentioned that she'd love to write about him, but didn't feel her writing would tell the story of what a wonderful horse, and friend, he'd been. I'd been looking for a new project, so I volunteered.

My writing world, with the exception of a few memoirs, generally spins in fiction, where I have fun creating new worlds, characters, and dialogue. I thought non-fiction would provide the challenge that many writers look for. It has. All I had to do was take the facts and weave them into a story that people will want to read. Not an easy task.

Originally, I thought the book would be just about "Sir Joey," — I've shortened his name to Joey for ease of typing — but as I learned about him and those who'd inhabited his world, the more I needed, and wanted, to know. Joey sent me on a quest to do just that. That mission has profoundly changed me and my outlook on life and people in ways that may be apparent only to me.

My welcome into the world of the horse was done without reservation or judgment. It's broadened my education, not only about equine professions, but about beliefs and views I'd not have understood if it weren't for Joey and his friends.

I invite you to know and love Joey, to share his life and times, and to revere his memory. You'll meet his friends — those who shared the barn or arena with him, or the cool, green pasture and the soft dirt and cool stream in Nutrioso, Arizona, that helped to momentarily relieve his painful feet — as well as others who populate the world of the horse.

You'll learn about communicating with animals. In fact, by the time you've finished reading this book, it's our intention that you'll have learned many things about the cord between the human and animal worlds which you may not have been aware. In Deb's words, "With the assistance of animals, we can help others gain a better understanding of how to learn and fulfill our soul's purpose."

Anyone who's loved animals, whether their preference is canine, equine, feline, porcine, or creatures without spines will relate to the love that bound a woman and a horse together; two souls who walked a journey, side by side.

Although I wish I'd known Joey as well as those who were able to share his life did — whether they be two-legged or four-legged — I'm grateful, and thankful, for what he's done for me.

Because of him, the population of my world is now inhabited by new friends — with two-legs and four — whom I treasure.

"Thank you, Sir Joey."

CHAPTER ONE
Joey's Morning

"As I stood in his stall that warm, November night in 2010, sending Sir Joey love and healing energy, I found myself going to his place of quiet, a place where he no longer felt the pain of his aching feet. At first, I saw him walking into a bubble that had an opalescent glow, then a second layer of pink appeared, representing his unconditional love; then a pasture of lush, green grass appeared, that not only served his grazing desires but the soft, damp earth that cushioned his feet with cooling relief.

(Photo by Deb Wood)

Joey had been running a fever for two weeks and had already taken the first series of antibiotics to fight the infection that showed up in his blood work. At this time, we still did not know where the infection was coming from.

Two years prior, Joey had an abscess in his right, rear foot. It took us over a year to locate its origin. At first, the infection tried to come out from the sole of his foot and then the coronary band. Both times, we thought he'd fully recovered only to find that he had a soft spot on the top of that foot — an inch wide and three inches deep — that needed to be drilled and drained. His back shoes were removed and never replaced. He was half way there!

Five years prior, he'd asked for his shoes to be removed because they caused him much discomfort. We honored his wishes. After several weeks of going "barefoot," he became so lame that we had no choice but to put his shoes back on, using pads because of his thin soles and flat feet.

With each passing year, we'd seen the pain in his eyes as his entire body flinched with every strike of the farrier's tool used to attach the shoes to his feet.

Also during that November night session with Joey, he'd told me that he wanted slippers on his feet. He was sure that we could find the ones that he needed that would support him enough so that he could be rid of metal shoes forever.

I remembered that I'd picked up a holistic handout at the feed store that had an ad for hoof pads that were designed to help horses transition from shoes to going barefoot. Lo and behold, when I checked the website they had slippers to hold the pads onto the horses' feet. There were the slippers that he'd asked for! I believe there are no coincidences and that we are divinely guided at all times — if we'd just take the time to listen.

Joey began progressing very well with his new hoof pads and slippers. I believe that while he was in his place of quiet, he was also divinely guided to show us how to assist him in the transition he so desperately desired: to spend the rest of his life not having to have shoes with nails. When he asked to have his shoes removed five years prior, these amazing products that were helping him so much had not existed.

Even though Joey was able to walk better with the help of the pads and slippers, his fever remained. Two months later, January's temperatures plunged and the wind-chill was just unbearable for his compromised immune system. The vet ran another series of blood tests, including cultures, which showed several different types of infection, and a particular antibiotic was chosen to help fight them all.

His digestion had slowed and he was given a major dose of oils to get things moving once again. He was beginning to colic from the pain. Once again, he moved through it and we continued to treat the infections.

Joey was adamant about not wanting to be put down. He feared that every shot that he received would be his last.

As hard as it was, we vowed to honor his decision and allow him to pass on his own, which he did on January 12, 2011.

In his final months, weeks, days and hours he continually showed me how to love with no boundaries, to accept everyone for who they are and not who or what I think they should be, to forgive me, to be more understanding and compassionate, and to love myself first. But Joey's specialty was to teach everyone to receive. He had finally learned that lesson for himself and he began to love receiving energy work, being groomed, along with every hug, kiss and compliment given.

Sir Joey is truly my hero as well as a hero to the many others who came to Wood Haven Healing Center to be in his presence. He was, and still is, a wonderful healer. His transformation was the most enlightening, heartwarming and spiritual event I've ever experienced."

These were Deb's thoughts, feelings, and emotions as she wrote them on the morning that Sir Joey crossed the Rainbow Bridge. (See the last chapter for its meaning).

She's sharing them with you as you begin your journey with Joey.

CHAPTER TWO
Meet Sir Joey

Deb said, "Joey was a one of kind black and white Paint. Standing proud and gallant, his unique markings caught the eyes of everyone who entered the barn at Wood Haven.

Joey was the glue, the strength, and the security for all the other horses here. Without question, they knew who was in charge and where they stood.

His presence was huge and so was his heart. He guided and supported anyone who asked for his help by showing them how they appeared to others.

Joey could easily read people from as far away as the front gate to the barn yard. He just knew and didn't have any problem making his reactions visible.

His knowledge and strength created a wonderful energy here. Many people came to Wood Haven just to be in his presence. Looking into his eyes would offer a gentle peace and hope for the moment as well as the future.

In Joey's final months, he brought forth a renewed spiritual awakening in me. It increased my hunger for knowledge; a way to find the whys and how's to grow within myself. A way to find the answers I had been searching for.

I believe that every horse that has come to us is a gift. In some realm of Spirit, we choose each other for reasons we are not aware of at the time.

Thank God for the gifts; thank God for our time with Sir Joey. It was a wonderful journey.

"It was our hearts that came together, providing healing for each other. We were not separate; we were *one*. That's how it works."

"Until one has loved an animal, part of one's soul remains unawakened."

Anatole France — 1844-1924

CHAPTER THREE
My Friend Joey

Rev. Dale A. Hallen D.M. of The Center of Hope in Tucson, Arizona, (see Contributor's page for his website) wrote: "Joey was an exceptional Creature and Teacher. He was my friend.

"It has always fascinated me that some people communicate so effortlessly with animals; they know what is being asked. Deb always seemed to know what Joey wanted and/or needed.

"Deb told me on several occasions that Joey was asking for 'that guy with the mustache.' I learned to listen to Joey and I was honored to share "my gifts" with him. I learned how to approach animals in a much more serene and sensitive manner.

"Joey showed me his appreciation for this sensitivity and caring. He responded very well to Reiki* and after his energetic adjustments, he looked at me with his glorious gaze as if to say, 'Thank You, I know you care about me.'

"Joey trusted those who cared for him, and he trusted and loved those who were brought out to Wood Haven for healing sessions.

"Joey has a forever place in my heart and in my being.

"Like all good friend and family members that have passed on, they remain with us in spirit and help to teach and guide in all we do and all we endeavor to be. I feel honored once again to think about and write about my friend, Joey."

*Reiki, as described by the International Center for Reiki Training is "a Japanese technique for stress reduction and relaxation that also promotes healing. It is administered by "laying on hands" and is based on the idea that an unseen "life force energy" flows through us and is what causes us to be alive. If one's life force energy is low, then we are more likely to get sick or feel stress, and if it is high, we are more capable of being happy and healthy.

The word Reiki is made of two Japanese words - *Rei* which means "God's Wisdom or the Higher Power" and *Ki* which is "life force energy." So Reiki is actually "spiritually guided life force energy."

CHAPTER FOUR
This Is Where Joey Lived

It's thirty-three round-trip miles from our house, in Tucson, Arizona, to Wood Haven Healing Center in Marana, Arizona.

As my husband, Doug, turned off of Interstate 10 onto the two-lane Avra Valley Road, my excitement would build. Our speed dropped from a scary 75 miles per hour to a turtle's crawl of somewhere between 35 and 45, which made me antsy; I wanted to get to the ranch!

The landscape intermittently changes from desert to cropland — cotton and alfalfa being the main crops — dotted here and there are fairly new subdivisions, new and older manufactured homes, and small businesses. Seemingly a hodgepodge, there *is* a community growing out here.

A variety of desert trees thrive on either side of the road, ranging from what looks to be deadwood in the winter, to lush foliage after the rains add their magic. This is what the Arizona desert looks like in our corner of the world. We who call it home are used to what some visitors might assess as "desolate." They've never witnessed the mystical change rain brings to the desert, seemingly overnight.

The remains of rugged, worn-down mountains stand sentinel far ahead of us; the tailings of Silverbell Mine are visible; we're 16 miles from Saguaro National Monument. Here and there plastic flowers — sun-bleached or new — are attached to small Styrofoam crosses, perpetuating the site where someone left this earth; red hawks lazily surf thermals, looking for their next meal.

My wanting to be at the ranch has become an addiction; much like I imagine addicts feel when thinking about their next score. I know that soon I'll experience a feeling of intense peace and tranquility.

Turning onto Anway — we're getting close; more trees now. A left turn onto Lambert Lane and mesquite trees greet us. Turn right onto Derringer and small ranch-style homes welcome us; another right onto Pepperbox and we're there!

Rocko, Shelby and Abbey, Deb's gorgeous, well-mannered Dalmatians race to greet us; Rocko's almost always the winner.

As the dogs accompany us to the barn, I look to see which horses are in the arena on our left — maybe Champ, or Dottie or Mama — Sapphire usually stays at an area in back of the barn with Annie and Sis, who are in another arena near her.

I love the barn. When it was built in 2004, Deb never dreamed it would become a Healing Center.

They named it "Wood Haven." As Deb's passion to help people, and animals, increased, the name evolved to Wood Haven Healing.

Her work helps guide her clients to find peace and joy in their lives by using Color and Light Therapy and, by way of the horses, teaching them techniques to move through emotional and physically crippling issues. Most of the time, it revolves around forgiveness of self and or others.

Sure, the barn houses the horses, but it's more than that; it's a safe harbor for me and the others who arrive daily as well. Its shelter provides immunity from the storms that life brings. The other worlds, the ones filled with a mixture of pain, fear, anxiety or daily folderol, are not allowed. This is a reserve for humans as well as horses, it's "sanctuary."

As you enter the barn, your eyes are drawn, arrow straight, to the open exit on the other end, which leads to corrals where Sapphire, Sis, and Annie, might be. Immediately to the right stand four dirt-floored stalls. A hinged portion of the wall at the stalls' rear that's generally open about half-way up, can easily be swung down when bad weather sets in.

On the left is a small, L-shaped living area, furniture invitingly arranged; walls painted blue-grey, matching the blue-grey painted concrete floor. A wooden table, featuring two wooden chairs on either of its sides, and two stools (one on each end) stand in the middle of an area carpet. The table, chair and stool legs are painted a dark green; a woven wooden basket filled with small rocks sits on top of a grey and white striped serape that covers the table. (A serape is a narrow rectangular blanket with fringed edges that was worn as a cape or shawl by men in northern Mexico and southern Arizona. In the last century it has become popular to use serapes for home fashions, such as wall hangings, throws, and table covers).

To the left of the table and chair arrangement, where Deb and I spent much of our time talking about horses, are two doors, also painted dark green. One leads to a bathroom, complete with shower; the other along the shortest side of the "L," leads outside to a patio, sporting comfortable furniture that overlooks more corrals and an arena.

A serape-covered couch stands against the wall. A small, curtain-covered window at ceiling height allows natural light, and underneath them hangs a dried flower wreath, a cross fashioned from horseshoes, and an angel.

A corner table holds a lamp; the base is fashioned out of horseshoes. The longest portion of the" L" features a large, light oak entertainment center, the shelves host a small stereo system and miscellaneous treasures, including a wagon wheel;

another serape-covered couch sits in front of the entertainment center.

Small birds flit in and out; sometimes landing on a girder, not staying long before they're on their way. Their joyful tweets and twitters lend a comforting sound to an already blissful atmosphere. During Christmas, the girders are wrapped with boughs and small, twinkling lights.

Everything is balanced. There's peace here.

This is where Sir Joey spent his last years before crossing over the Rainbow Bridge. (See last chapter for the story of the Rainbow Bridge).

Although those years were filled with pain, they were definitely filled with *love*.

I visited the ranch often to do the research necessary to tell its story. Although, at first, getting to know the horses was integral to being able to tell their stories, I was not consciously aware of how I felt when I was with them. Slowly, as I got to know each one, it became profoundly obvious to me that during times of stress, if I'd concentrate on nothing but being with them, I'd become calm and serene. I wonder if they're aware of the power they possess.

CHAPTER FIVE
Joey's Early Years

The whinnying of horses, the lowing of cattle; the smell of hay, manure and sweat from both animals and humans, the sun's heat propelling the temperatures to 90° and beyond; the dust — throat-clutching, dry-spitting dust from the constant moving of hooves. This pretty much describes the noisy feed lot in West Texas where a horse trader found four-year old Joey during a buying trip in 1992.

He'd purchased five horses which he was going to transport to Tucson, Arizona to sell. After he'd loaded the five into his six-stall horse trailer, he spotted Joey. Something about the way Joey stood and looked at him made him decide to purchase an even half-dozen horses.

That's the way it was with Joey; there was always that "special something" that humans responded to. He'd traveled a long, painful road before being able to help those who came to Wood Haven Healing Center; before sharing his life with his diminutive, special, loving friend, Deb Wood.

In 1998, Deb saw signs in a hardware store in Avra Valley, advertising a horse for sale. Deb went to see him and, after riding him and seeing how sweet and kind he could be, she told her husband, Bill, about him. They bought him on Valentine's Day.

Soon after he arrived, Joey began to show signs of being very uncomfortable while being ridden and he became grouchy. Deb believes that it was the pain in his legs and feet that caused him to act out.

Unaware at that time of the problems Joey had with his feet, which would plague him for the rest of his life, Deb and Bill both rode him for a while, enjoying trail riding in the desert before Deb eventually rode him in trail pattern competition in area horse shows. Eventually, the twisting moves aggravated his feet; quarter cracks appeared in the coronary areas and he was unable to continue performing. Thereafter, Bill rode him only on flat terrain where no twisting was necessary.

They found out that he had White Line Disease, which creates a soft, chalky tissue on the bottom of his hoof. A complete checkup by a vet, including X-rays, established that he had high and low ringbone, followed by quarter cracks.

Mike Gorczyca, a solid man, was Joey's farrier, and hero. He helped Joey's feet to heal as best he could, but more about Mike later on. You'll like him.

The Woods would later learn that prior to their purchasing Joey, he'd been the "head" horse in team roping, also known as heading and heeling competition.

I'll explain this competition so that you'll know what Joey was called upon to do in this regard.

The heading and heeling event features a steer and two riders. The steers are moved from a holding corral through a series of narrow runways leading to the roping arena. The runways keep the steers in a single file and one at a time they are moved to a chute with spring-loaded door in front (a solid gate behind) so that only one steer is released at a time.

On each side of the chute is an area called the box, that's big enough for a horse and rider. Let's presume that, in our case, Joey would usually stand on the left side (if his rider was right-handed) and wait for his rider to "call" for the steer. A taut rope, called the barrier, ran in front of the header's box and was fastened to an easily released rope on the neck of the steer. (Its length is designed to ensure that the steer gets a head start).

When the rider called for the steer, an assistant pulled a lever which opened the chute doors and it was Joey's job to run hell-bent-for-election after the steer so that his rider could rope the steer in one of three catches: either around both horns, or a neck catch or a half-head catch (around the neck and one horn). The rider then took a "dally" (wrapping the rope a couple of times around the horn of his saddle) turned Joey to the left, with the steer following still running, allowing the heeler to throw a loop of rope to catch the running steer's hind legs. As soon as the heeler "dallied" tight, Joey would be turned so that he faced the steer and the heeler, then he and the other horse would back up slightly to stretch out the steer's hind legs, immobilizing it.

When that happened, an official waved a flag, the time was noted and the steer was released.

A professional-level team takes between four and twelve seconds to stretch the steer, depending on the length of the arena. A team may take longer, particularly if the heeler misses the first throw and has to try again.

Apparently, Joey did some barrel racing too. To me, this event requires a horse to do phenomenal things. It's a combination of a horse's athletic ability and mental condition and the skills of the rider to safely and successfully maneuver through a clover leaf pattern around three barrels (typically fifty-five gallon metal or plastic drums) placed in a triangle in the center of an arena. The ground (quality, depth, type of sand or dirt) also plays a big part.

The point is to make a run as fast as possible, while the time is clocked by an electronic eye, or by a judge who manually takes the time using a sharp eye and a flag to let the clocker know when to hit the timer stop (usually used in local and non-professional events).

When I've watched these events, I always held my breath until the race was finished.

The time begins when the horse and rider cross the starting line, and ends when the barrel pattern has been successfully accomplished and the horse and rider cross the finish line.

At first, this was an event for women, and early on the pattern alternated between a figure-eight and a cloverleaf, but the "8" was eventually dropped in favor of the cloverleaf.

Entering the arena at top speed through the center entrance (or alley if in a rodeo arena) the electronic timer beam is crossed by horse and rider. The timer keeps running until the beam is crossed again at the end of the run.

Barrel-racing horses not only need to be fast, they need strength and agility to get through the course in as little time as possible. A horse that is able to hug the barrels as well as quickly and accurately follow directions will be a horse with consistently low time.

The approach to the first barrel is critical to a successful pattern. The rider must rate their horse's speed at the right moment so they can make a perfect turn. The turns should be an even half -circle around the barrel. As the horse readies to make the turn, the rider must be in a good position as well, meaning sitting deep in the saddle, using one hand on the horn and the other hand guiding the horse through and around the barrel.

The rider's legs should be held close to the horse's sides; the leg to the inside of the turn should be held securely along the girth to support the horse's rib cage and give them a focal point for the turn. The physical fitness of the rider and the horse must be optimal to avoid injury to both. Protective boots for the horse's legs are a must.

I've always been impressed by the stamina of the horse's legs and feet. If you watch the event, look at the angle that the horse's legs and hooves take as they round the barrel.

When approaching the second barrel, the rider will be looking through the turn, focusing on the new spot to enter the second barrel, which is across the arena. The horse and rider will go around this barrel in the opposite direction, following the same procedure, just switching to the opposite limbs. Next, running toward the backside of the arena opposite to the entrance and through the middle, then heading for the third and final barrel that they must turn, in the same direction the second barrel was taken, all the while racing against the timer.

Completing the third and final turn sends them heading for home, which represents crossing the timer, or line, once more to finish (and allowing me to breathe once more). Watching a horse and rider who are in complete sync no matter what they're doing together is simultaneously frightening and beautiful.

The fastest time wins. Not all horses start from the right barrel; some start from the left barrel. Riders usually let their horses pick which is more comfortable.

The price for the purchase of a high quality barrel-racing horse may reach over $100,000.00, depending upon the ability of the horse. Breeding plays a part in the horse's sale price, but athletic ability, intelligence, drive and *willingness to please* also play a bit part.

If that's all it takes, then I believe Joey's price would have been astronomical, because he was all heart. *Pleasing humans* was what he lived for. As Deb puts it, "he gave everything he had, no matter what he was doing."

Joey also knew what *he* wanted. During one particular competition set up with obstacles, horses are expected to step over logs placed in a certain formation. The horses are graded by points given for each obstacle conquered. One day, using his back leg, he moved the logs around one by one until the box was the size he wanted so he was able to move around in the square created by the logs.

After Deb learned to communicate with animals, Joey (whom Deb initially nicknamed "Slow Joe Schmo from Kokomo," because he walked so slowly) officially became Sir Joey. During a meditation session with him, Deb saw him being used as a jousting horse for a royal family in a past life. During his last joust, Joey fell and was euthanized.

Joey communicated to Deb that falling not only shamed him, but also shamed his Royal family. The shame he felt followed him into this life, which Deb believes gave him a poor foundation — his feet. To help him overcome his past, she immediately renamed him "Sir Joey."

His transformation began when he was shown forgiveness; after Deb told him to let go of his past; to forgive himself.

Deb: "Fear of failing is strong in many people and causes emotional problems which can lead to physical problems."

Soon, "Sir Joey" wanted to do "healing work" and began to move through many phases at Wood Haven.

Barbara and Dave Lorenz remember the effect Joey had on them. Barbara relates:

"Joey sensed people in need of healing.

Dave has had a chronic pain in his neck and back for ten years after a fall. He came to the barn to do a healing meditation with Deb when [unbidden] Joey came from his open stall and walked over to

Dave. As soon as Joey stood next to him, Dave felt a warm vibration in his neck and saw a pink color within his entire body … a feeling of calmness and release.

Being a Reiki Master, Dave understood about the healing vibration that was enhanced when Joey's energy came near him. Joey just stood quietly for probably ten minutes, then slowly walked back to his stall.

Dave opened his eyes, and felt no pain, something that had not happened for months. Joey had sensed his deep-seated pain and brought his own special vibration of healing into Dave's energy field and the energy flowed where it was needed most.

It was amazing. As healers ourselves, we saw the power of unconditional love and healing through the love of this amazing horse: Joey."

Barbara and Dave are both Reiki Masters, and are trained in the International Center for Reiki methods, using the traditional Usui method of Reiki.

CHAPTER SIX

Meet Deb Wood

Deb remembers, "I know that I have been guided and protected by guardian angels all my life. My life's choices have always seemed simple to me. The childhood I am about to describe reflects the simple things in life; a life that required lots of hard work, while living off the earth, and the assurance of never ending love from family. These simple things shaped my life and mean so very much to me.

I have always loved the outdoors and animals. As far back as I can remember, I have felt such a compassion for animals. The love our pets give unconditionally is like no other. I've always felt connected to them in a very special way and I have come to understand that *trust* is the reason for the deep connection; for them, the trust that they will always be taken care of. For us, the trust knowing that as long as they are with us we will be loved, protected and comforted. NO MATTER WHAT!

My grandma and grandpa always had a dog, cats and sometimes even puppies. The happy tails greeting me when I arrived always made my heart sing. Of course, I always wanted to take them in the house with me, but Grandma wouldn't allow that. However, I soon found that if I kept one on my lap I could sit on the landing between the kitchen and the basement steps and watch Grandma happily working in the kitchen.

As I close my eyes, I can still smell the wonderful food she loved to prepare. I know that everything she made was from her heart. From homemade pies, to noodles, soup, and the best fried chicken in Preble County, Ohio!

My Grandma had two plates hanging in her kitchen. One stated the Golden Rule *"Do unto others as you would have others do unto you"*. The other was the Lord's Prayer, on a beautiful white scalloped plate trimmed with gold edges and letters. Those plates were always there, even after the kitchen was painted over and over again. They were hung as a constant reminder to all who entered the kitchen.

After all, that room was the most important room in the house. It was there at the kitchen table, that the daily events were shared, plans were made and dreams were spoken. And as I reminisce and write my stories, I can see how this type of consistency shaped my life.

My Friend Flicka: what wonderful heartfelt family stories that made me cry and smile all in one program. And on the weekends we enjoyed *The Ed Sullivan Show* and *Lawrence Welk*. While watching TV on Saturday nights we always had popcorn.

TV was something that was enjoyed mainly in the evenings because there was so much work to be done during the day. I spent a lot of my childhood with my wonderful grandparents enjoying the outside and working with them in the garden and truck patch they nourished every summer. It was then that I cultivated my own garden of loving memories.

Grandma's huge garden and truck patch had a border of marigolds and zinnias. Their odor kept unwanted pests away. All planted so carefully by hand, the rainbow of color was a sight to see for everyone passing by.

There were strawberries, green beans, cabbage, onions, lima beans, carrots, lettuce, tomatoes, corn, pumpkin, banana squash, potatoes, watermelon, cucumbers, yellow squash, peas, kale and rhubarb. The strawberries were made into what Grandma called 'dope for ice cream topping' as well as for pie and short cake.

The cucumbers were used to can the ever-so thin bread and butter pickles. I can still hear the sounds of the pressure cooker preparing all the garden fresh food to be enjoyed during those long winter months ahead. The basement chest freezers were filled with what could be frozen and the cold cellar shelves were lined with the produce she'd canned.

Grandpa was in charge of the meat department. He and his brothers butchered their own home grown beef and pork, which was divided within the families and frozen as well. Grandma also had chickens and a rooster who loved to chase me as I neared the house. But it was Grandma to the rescue with broom in hand to settle the score. Even though the rooster was a pain in my backside we always had fresh eggs and fresh chicken!

Grandpa always made sure there was a cold watermelon in the fridge or homemade ice cream in the freezer for us to enjoy after dinner on those relaxing summer nights. Not only did *we* enjoy the benefits of all the fresh fruits and vegetables, but neighbors, friends and other relatives would come to the barn where there were tables of tomatoes, corn, onions and potatoes for the sharing.

The property was lined with huge cedar trees and during the summer we enjoyed snowball and lilac bushes, and Great Grandma's beautiful rose garden. One of greatest memories is that of the natural spring that ran on the Swain Road property all year long. That old metal trough continually supplied water for all the animals, plants and residents there. There were always glass jars of that wonderful, crystal clear, ice cold water in the fridge. That natural spring still runs today, taking care of all things in need.

Even though it's been forty years, I can still remember waking up in my great grandmother's bedroom, and seeing the light-green colored walls. I can also remember the placement of all the furniture, the beautiful wood floors, the floral curtains blocking the morning sun and the smell of Grandma's pancakes, with her homemade maple syrup. Also, the sound of peacocks from the neighbors up the road, and the cooing of doves just outside my window were such soothing sounds to start a new day.

As I grew older and wanted to talk on the phone to my school friends, I had to make sure no one else was on the line in the neighborhood. Needless to say, if I had something personal to talk about, like the cute boy that sat next to me on the bus, I didn't use the phone! The prefix for that area was 456 but everyone said 'GL6' and then the rest of the number. Our number there was GL6-2924.

The neatest thing worth mentioning about the phone system was if someone needed someone to talk to, they just dialed O and the operator was always there and knew everyone in Preble County!

The bread man made once-a-week deliveries in our rural area. Grandma always had pennies for me to buy Tootsie Rolls™ that the bread man kept in a wooden drawer in the back of his delivery truck. Sunbeam Bread™ was painted on the blue and yellow truck with a picture of a young blonde girl enjoying a slice of bread. That was really a treat, because candy was about the only thing that was *not grown* on the property and we had quite a drive to go to get it.

Every holiday was celebrated here with our entire family: grandparents, parents, sister and brother, aunts, uncles, cousins and great grandmas too. In the winter the windows would be covered with moisture because of the old radiators used for heating and all the food being prepared to serve thirty people.

Of course, Christmas Eve was the greatest of all. Grandma made at least six different types of pies to fill all requests! At Thanksgiving everyone drew a name of someone to buy or make a Christmas gift for. That was a simple, beautiful time of my life, when I saw everyone coming together for fellowship and honest family joy.

My Uncle Hubert lived just a half mile up the road and I would love to walk there to ride his ponies. Ponder was a brown and white gelding and we were inseparable during the summers. I remember one August, Uncle Hubert hauled Ponder to the Preble County Fair so I could ride him in the parade. What a thrill! I thought I looked so cool in my shorts, boots and cowgirl hat. My Grandpa had given me a soda pop to drink right before the parade started so it was a *very long* parade if you know what I mean.

I would also take Ponder down to the creek bottom to ride and he would buck me off *a lot*. I can remember lying on the ground and Grandpa saying, "Get up and get back on." Gasping for air, I did get back on, and off we'd go again. After riding I would bathe him and take him home. That, my friends, was the beginning of my love for horses.

While down by the creek, we gathered black walnuts. I can still see Grandma sitting on the basement floor with the walnuts that had been drying on newspaper, using a hammer to open the shell and crush the nuts to put in her next spice cake. Now, they come in bags already crushed and shelled, right?

My sister, brother and I would frequently spend Saturday nights with Grandma and Grandpa. Grandma being the sport she was, allowed us to sneak up behind her while she was doing dishes and place wooden clothes pins and fishing lures on her apron hem line. We would all run to hide and she would pretend she didn't know until she walked away from the sink to grab another pan to wash. We didn't need much to be entertained at that age. Just laughs and hugs suited us just fine.

It is no wonder I wanted to play the saxophone in the school band. My Grandpa and my dad both played tenor sax. I'm sure hearing it while in the womb helped that along as well as remembering Grandpa practicing in the basement. What wonderful sounds of love and joy oozing up through those old wooden floors on Swain Road. Grandpa, Uncle Hubert and Uncle Stanley formed a band called "Clark's Combo." They played at dances, parties and family gatherings. Grandpa never read music. He had a wonderful gift to play by ear. Just hearing music was all he needed to join in and play a song completely and exactly.

As I neared driving age—well, I think Grandpa let me start about twelve—he would drive the car up the road and over the bridge, then I got to drive to a little market several miles away for milk. Once we got to the bridge again, Grandpa would take the wheel and drive home. Once inside the house we would sit down for dinner, ready to take that first bite, and Grandma would say, "You let her drive, didn't you?" Busted! But Grandpa sweetly said, "Now, Ida, we didn't pass another car on the road." And that was the end of it. Until the next trip of course!

I can honestly say that I never heard my grandparents argue. Not one time in all the years I spent with them did I hear a cross word. Again, another constant in my life that showed me their love and respect for each other. I always felt comfort and joy.

There was an old barn on the property that was used for hay storage, cattle, draft horse stalls and a corn crib. The horses were used in the fields before the tractor appeared. Many hours were spent making tunnels in the stacked hay, searching for litters of kittens tucked safely away by their mothers and picking field corn off the cob just for something different to do. Grandpa had an old grey and red Ford tractor that I used to ride in the fields with him. Many hours were spent driving around the fields with him and me loving every minute of it! I was truly a tomboy with my Daisy™ BB gun in tote, which I requested for one of my birthdays.

My final story is about my favorite Christmas. I was in Junior High and my parents, sister, brother, and I had just returned home from the family gathering at my grandparents' home. It was around midnight, Christmas Eve. As we were getting ready for bed we could hear bells ringing outside. As we opened the front door and turned on the porch light we could see a horse standing in the front yard. It was Kelle, the Quarter Horse mare I had ridden all summer on a farm not far from our house.

She was decorated with a silver bow around her fat tummy, swollen in foal, with red velvet on her bridle. Oh yes, I cried! It was the most special Christmas gift ever. My own horse! That particular night, there was a full moon and the owners of the farm that delivered her, and my family, followed behind me as I rode Kelle back down the road back to the farm where she would stay.

It was snowing and we were all singing Christmas Carols on the three-mile ride to the farm. That story, along with the summer I spent with Kelle prior to Christmas, was written and published in Readers Digest around 1970. I enjoyed Kelle for many years competing in 4-H and open shows in Ohio. But the greatest times were just her and I riding through the woods, creeks and snow, just enjoying each other's company. In Junior High, when I received Kelle, my best friend was my horse. What more could a girl want?

I hope you have enjoyed my memories. I am so fortunate to have had such a wonderful, loving, simple life as a child. In this day and time of electronics, internet, and all sorts of stimulating distractions, I hope you are inspired to take the time to find and enjoy the simple things in your life; time to embrace them and value their importance. Life is precious and can be so simple. It is all about choices. Choose to have a good day, week, month, year and life!"

***

In 1984, after moving to Tucson with her first husband, Deb worked as an aerobics instructor with many of the YMCAs in Tucson, as well as a cardiopulmonary therapist at the Fitness Institute of Tucson, in the downtown area.

After marrying Bill in 1993, she again turned to the 4-H organization that she'd begun working with in Ohio. Working hard as a volunteer for fifteen years and eventually holding many of the posts in that organization, she switched to working with people and horses in a different way.

Have you ever questioned your role in life? Why you're here? What's your life path? Deb always had.

In 2005, she attempted to find answers, and began a new life journey and enlightened spiritual path, learning about things that many scoff at, for instance: Reiki, Angelic Healing, Animal Communication, and Color and Light Therapy.

After attending many levels of Animal Communications with Linda Johns, of *Journey to Healing,* she began to understand the human and animal connection for finding inner peace. But first, she had to learn to peel off layers of inhibitions — much like peeling an onion — and let her eyes be opened to what was being taught. Until she worked with her own horses, she felt she'd never be able to communicate with animals.

Her certification for Color and Light Therapy was with Lynn Younger of Sedona, Arizona. She also holds certifications in Reflexology for people and Reiki, which she uses in sessions for people and animals.

At Wood Haven Healing she's found that Colorpuncture Light Work not only benefits her human clients, but has a beneficial effect on her horses and other animals as well. By focusing on energetic pathways, or designated acupuncture points, the biophysics of light show that light and color restore proper cellular communication, supporting the body's many detoxification and healing processes.

Colorpuncture has been scientifically shown to offer relief in other acute and chronic conditions. Since different colors of light carry different vibrations, each sequence will have specific results and can target different concerns .Depending upon the animal's or the person's particular needs, the sequences are individually designed to calm and/or strengthen and are most effective when targeted to:

- Relieve skin conditions like hot spots or injuries and wounds
- Detoxify by flushing out stored poisons or medications
- Activate a sense of well-being and peace by shifting physical and emotional blockages
- Rebuild energy in degenerative or geriatric conditions

- Ease joint or spinal pain and relieve arthritic inflammations
- Support the immune system and address chronic allergic reactions

Along with these acquired tools, she allows her intuition to guide her in applying and teaching those techniques that are needed to promote the releasing and clearing of old memory patterns (physical or emotional), which in turn helps her clients to find joy, peace, harmony, understanding, and physical wellness.

She believes healing comes about when the condition or cause of an illness is addressed and transformed. If healing goes no farther than a mere relief or masking of the symptoms, then eventually that which brought about the need for healing in the first place, will resurface and manifest itself in one form or another.

Life lessons taught at Wood Haven include:
- Accepting that the only person you can change is yourself
- Choosing to have a wonderful day, week, month, year and life
- Becoming more loving of yourself and others
- Letting go of things you cannot control
- Appreciating what you have

- Understanding where your anger and fear come from
- Forgiving yourself and others
- Acknowledging your self-worth

A childhood friend of Deb's, Carol Orr Byrum, told me that "Between 1970-1974, in the small, quaint town of Lewisburg, Ohio, Debbie Clark Wood and I went to Twin Valley North High School. There were less than four hundred students in the whole school! We both played sports together, although she was much more the athlete. She was good at everything she did. She was pretty, smart, and friendly; everyone who knew her liked her.

"We shared a love of horses. I lived on five acres outside of town in West Sonora; she lived on the other side of town and boarded her horse at a farm near Verona. We both were competitive; the only difference was she was coordinated and I wasn't! On the weekends we would show our horses at different local venues and some of the times we competed against each other; she usually won. But we had fun and always remained friends.

"Our lives were similar as we were both popular in school; during prom she was voted Queen and I was second runner up. If I'm not mistaken she was voted "Most Popular" and I was voted "Most Athletic" which was funny as I tried to play everything but was a klutz.

"I got married right out of high school and moved out of Lewisburg and lost touch with everyone until Facebook, where Deb and I reconnected.

"In June 2011, I was diagnosed with a very aggressive form of breast cancer called "Triple Negative." Deb, as well as most of the girls I graduated with supported and encouraged me through my chemo and radiation even though I had not seen them in over thirty-seven years. "Deb always commented on my progress with prayers, words of endearment, inviting me to Arizona to visit and rest, ride ... as she knows how much a horse can change your life.

"After all these years she is still there for me like time had not passed at all. I thank God for her; she has a special soul about her and I am happy to call her friend and have her in my life."

CHAPTER SEVEN
Meet Bill Wood

Tall, sandy-haired, square-jawed, solid, Bill is Deb's rock and partner in all things. It's obvious that they're still very much in love after twenty years. You don't have to be around them for too long before you realize that if ever two people were meant for each other, it's these two.

As a boy, living around St. Louis, Missouri, his family had several ponies. They used to vacation in Tucson and in 1970 they moved there. He "knocked around" for a bit before working for a several plumbing companies, and he said the "rest is history."

In 1979 Bill began his own company — "Wood's Plumbing" — and a better plumber you'll never find. This is an unsolicited endorsement after our experience with them.

They're on call twenty-four/seven, which was obvious on the Sunday I interviewed him. We paused our chat so that he could answer a phone call from a woman needing a plumber *right now*. He immediately contacted his son, Wes, who took the call and saved that lady's day.

Bill bought the property the ranch sits on in 1983, sold it, then re-bought it ten years later when he and Deb married. They added the barn and other outbuildings soon after when the horses started arriving!

During our conversation, he said, *"people should learn more about horses before they decide to have them."* (I emphasized those words so you'll know how strongly he feels about that). He added, "There is a lot more to caring for a horse than just feeding it. For instance, they have tricky digestive systems."

When he spoke about Joey, his voice often became tender; he'd chuckle as he remembered things about him; but at other times I got the feeling that his speaking about Joey was difficult for him:

"Joey reached out to me. He was my rock. I didn't realize how much pain he was in." Then, he laughed as he remembered what a joker Joey could be. "He could be ornery, but he was playful, too."

To prove his point, he said, "One day when I was working on a project, Joey was walking around and came to see what I was doing. The next thing I knew Joey had grabbed me on the back of my neck — gently — and held on, then began to drool. I felt he was teasing me, but I think he wanted to see what my reaction would be. From then on, we were buddies."

Bill found out that when Joey was a roping horse, he drank beer. He'd pick up the bottle by the neck and swig it back. He loved to bite at watches and rings.

I'd wondered about the relationship between Joey and those wonderful Dalmatians they have. He explained that the dogs felt very comfortable with him; they'd lie under his feet. But, it was Rocko with whom the connection was the strongest.

Bill described Rocko (who's my favorite), as the helper, but all of the dogs are there for Deb's protection.

As we talked, he told me a little bit about each horse and their personalities. We'll explore each one in depth later on, but for now:

"Champ does things that Joey used to do - always the tease!"

"Dottie was a handful until Deb began using Color and Light Therapy to balance her hormones. Then she began to calm down."

"Mama and Sapphire, both quiet and settled mares, were donated by friends to assist Deb in her work with 4-H Club members. They now help Deb with her healing work."

"Sis is like a Chihuahua. She's little and wants to be "Number One," so she pushes the other horses around. Literally. She loves to do that to Champ. When the two of them are in the arena together, she'll get next to Champ and tries to bump his rump with hers. As she's quite a bit smaller, rump bumping really means just shoving him. He allows her to push him around; he'd never hurt her.

Deb and Bill sometimes ride at Catalina State Park, north of Tucson. There's an equestrian center there where you can stay overnight; they have stalls for the horses.

"Dottie's afraid of bees and hates flies. One day when I was riding her, a bee flew around and she panicked. She spun around trying to get rid of the bee and tossed me off, but I landed on my feet and got high marks from the people we were riding with."

Bill then repeated something I've heard time and again from just about everyone I spoke with while writing about Joey: "A horse never forgets kindness or abuse. They never let you down and they never stop loving."

Bill got quiet before saying, "Joey was in pain, but he clung to life, no matter what. He didn't want to leave us. We watched him rebound back time after time for ten years. We know in our hearts that he is with us, always has been and always will be."

And that's how it should be.

CHAPTER EIGHT
Meet the Horses of Wood Haven

SUNDIE GIRL was a sorrel Quarter-Horse, registered with the American Quarter Horse Association, who came from Green Valley, Arizona. This beauty was purchased for Bill to ride. At first, they believed she was eighteen years old, but it was discovered that she was closer to twenty-five.

She crossed over the Rainbow Bridge five years ago, one day shy of being thirty-three.

ANNIE and **SIS** initially brought tears to my eyes, followed with smiles, from the first day I met them. You can't talk about one, without talking about the other. Actually, I met Sis (age five) first — all thirty-nine brown and white inches of her. She came to the fence I was standing behind to check me over. Annie, who stands fifteen hands high, and whom Sis guards and protects from everything and every being, stood farther out in the corral. I'd have to pass inspection by her little guardian before meeting her.

ANNIE, a.k.a. **Annabelle Leigh**, age twenty-four: is a brown and white Paint, Deb's retired show horse and the only one who's won Deb a belt buckle. When Annie was preparing for shows, she enjoyed the bubble baths and the treats that were her rewards. Deb says she was a sight to see when competing on the trail classes; their thoughts were connected; they were in synch.

Seeing an ad in the paper, announcing "Paint Mare for sale," they went to see her; Bill fell in love with her and brought her home. At first, she was fearful of people and easily spooked.

Prior to Annie's arrival at Wood Haven, she'd had a foal who was sold when it was about a year old; she mourned for it, and was lonely. Deb was able to contact that foal (who was in the White Mountains at the time) who communicated to Deb that she was happy.

Although Annie was relieved to hear that news, during a meditation with Deb, she related that she wanted a companion horse, whose name was to be "Sis," and who was to look just like Annie. At a horse rescue ranch a couple of months later, Deb saw a horse who matched that description, although her name was Ginger. She was one of three miniature horses that had just arrived, but the only one who was colored the same as Annie — brown with white spots.

Deb had no other option, and from the moment Ginger (now renamed Sis per Annie's wish) arrived at Wood Haven, the two horses became inseparable; no horse, or human, is allowed near Annie, unless they've been okayed by Sis. She pretty much runs the place, and enjoys pushing the gelding, Champ, around. He'll suffer that indignity from no other horse.

Sis takes her job of protecting her companion quite seriously, so during my first meeting with Sis, while she tried to eat the silk roses from my cane, she was also determining what my interest was in Annie, and whether or not I would be allowed to get near her. This would happen in an astonishing, mystical way, during another visit, when Sis "allowed" me to get close to both of them at the same time.

During that visit, I was leaning against the bars of Annie's stall in the barn, my hands on either side of her head as I talked to her, when Deb said, "Close your eyes. I want you to try to connect to her."

I closed my eyes and stood quietly, still holding onto Annie, not knowing what to expect. I felt serene, forgetting the fact that standing is more often than not, a painful proposition for me.

At first I *saw* nothing. Then, it began. Slowly, brilliant blue streaks flashed, followed by a large patch of intense, cobalt blue.

I reported all of this to Deb, who said something like, "Just let it happen."

I say "something like" because I was so astonished at all of this that I wasn't concentrating on the words Deb was saying to me, only on what was happening between me and Annie.

Slowly, a form began to emerge. At first I saw just an outline of a horse's head and neck, which gradually morphed into a solid horse-profile that turned the color of cinnamon brown mixed with gold. It was a truly beautiful inner eye picture.

When I reported this to Deb, she quietly told me that my chakra had aligned with Annie's; our hearts had joined. I was elated. (Chakras are energy centers in the body. Animals and humans have them.)

But what happened next is something I never expected and something I will remember all of my life.

A gentle, soft, but insistent nudging from under my left arm signaled the arrival of Sis, whose head was now next to my cheek Although she'd been strolling in and out of the barn from the time I'd arrived, I'd been so deep in concentration that I hadn't heard her clop up.

A feeling of warmth spread through my entire body as the three of us stood, locked into a solid, harmonious triangle — me to Annie, Annie to Sis and Sis back to me — for I don't know how long. All I knew was that I was at peace; pain free; comfortable in the stillness of a moment that I didn't want to end — ever.

I said something like, "Thanks, Sis, for approving me and letting me in." 'Something like' because once more I was only concentrating on what I was feeling at the time, not on the actual words I was saying to this-just-a-tad-taller-than-three-feet wonder who was leaning against me.

Deb says Annie likes "energy work," likes to be touched and likes to work with children, especially those who are abused and neglected; she's able to pick them out of a crowd. However, Annie also loves mesquite beans, which hang from mesquite trees in pods and must be quite tasty, despite not being a good thing for her digestive system. She's also taught Champ how to check the trees for them.

Although the twenty-two mesquite trees on the property provide shade from Arizona's relentless sun, they keep Deb and her assistant on a constant hunt for fallen beans which must be raked to prevent the peptic problems inherent with their consumption.

Thank you, Annie and Sis. No matter the fact that Batman and Robin have been called the *Dynamic Duo* for years, you two will be known to me as the *Terrific Twosome*.

DOTTIE – age thirteen -- was donated to the Woods when she was in foal. She also had one other condition – *anger*. They found out she'd first been bred at two, then again at three, because it was thought it would "settle" her, but some experts consider those ages too young.

Her hormones were out of balance, but breeding her was not the answer.

Soon after arriving at Wood Haven, Dottie foaled Champ, and Deb treated her with Color and Light Therapy to rebalance her hormones, and her anger dissipated.

CHAMP, a Paint, age nine years, at first was named Squirt. He's always been a challenge. Deb says that because of their size, horses need boundaries.

To assist him to "grow up," Deb changed his name to Champ, which helped.

Champ has mirrored Deb's emotions — she doesn't like change and neither does he. If he's put into a different stall, he becomes upset. Although her biggest connection is with her mares, it's the geldings who've taught her the most. Champ taught her patience, to work as a team, to learn to let go of control and not to allow herself to react to other people's emotions.

Handsome Champ (he loves to hear the word handsome), has a striking white blaze — which he seems to have gotten from his mom, Dottie — with a coat the color of burnished copper in the sun. When he's viewed from his right side his eye is brown. But, when viewed from his left side, all else is the same, except for his left eye, which is light blue, with a black cornea.

This type of eye is a genetic anomaly (his father and sister both have blue eyes), and makes him seem ferocious. It's been said that horses who have two differently colored eyes can see between both worlds: our world and the spiritual world.

Joey and Champ were the first animals Deb began "listening" to. We'll be getting to that part of the story shortly.

SAPPHIRE, age twenty-six: is a sorrel mare Quarter-Horse, who, along with Mama is used for everything by kids and adults, from just plain riding to healing. After Sundie Girl passed, Deb needed a horse for her 4-H kids to ride, and Sapphire was offered as a donation. Deb communicated to Sapphire that she was welcome to stay if she agreed to give rides to children, which this sweet horse indicated was no problem.

Sweet describes Sapphire perfectly. The first time I met her, she was standing in a small, corral in the back of the barn, wearing a fly mask (which is more common than not).

I stand five feet even, and because of several spine surgeries, it's difficult for me to look up. But I wanted to get to know all of the horses, so I just began talking to Sapphire as I patted the side of her face. Slowly, she lowered her head and what happened next brings tears to my eyes even now. This wonderful, sweet horse was pressing her forehead ever so gently against my forehead.

A feeling of tranquility, mixed with happy, steadily seeped through me, from head to feet. I didn't want to move; I didn't want that feeling to end. If I had to ascribe a color to that feeling, I'd say "golden."

I quietly said, "Deb? What is she doing?"

Deb's answer: "She wants you to know she feels your pain."

I didn't know how to react to that. I've been in pain since 1997, when I was diagnosed with Degenerative Disk Disease, and began the first of six surgeries to my spine, not including the replacement of both hips. I'm not looking for sympathy here. I rely on medication for help, but it doesn't do the job completely, so I deal with it, and move on. It is what it is.

But just for that moment, I wasn't feeling any pain.

As Sapphire moved her head away, I felt a huge rush of love for this beautiful animal. I knew that from then on, every time I met her, I'd feel the same way.

MAMA, age 26, was donated to Wood Haven because she didn't like trailer loading. In order to help Mama understand that she could release her fear of being in a trailer, Deb worked in the trailer with her for three days, using blue hay bags, blue blankets, anything blue, to calm her. The color blue is thought to be calming to the soul in stressful situations. After three days, Deb heard her say, "I really prefer turquoise." Deb found Mama a turquoise halter, Mama decided to release her fear, she loaded, and was now able to go on distance rides and enjoy the kids.

Several days later, Deb entered the barn and communicated, "Hello beautiful."

Mama communicated, "Look at my face; my scars. I'm not beautiful."

Deb responded, "Everyone here has a scar of some kind, that's why we are here together — we are equal." Mama now believes she is truly beautiful because she is told that daily!

I wondered how long it takes for people to become healed. Deb told me, "There is no time line. It takes what it takes; it is what it is."

She figures that the horses have helped about fifty people, so far. At first, most people have to overcome their fear of horses; to get rid of fears that have been passed from generation to generation by those who've not been around horses that much — me included ("don't stare at horses; don't get too close").

This is done by initially having the clients groom the horses, feeling their energy through touching them, picking up their hooves, doing all of this while conquering their fear, whatever that fear may be.

Both young and old are helped to move through their emotional issues — fear, trauma, learning to forgive — if they are willing to receive the lessons that the horses offer.

The words "calm," "peace," "serene" and "tranquil" are used a lot in this book. Few adjectives describe the feeling that I, and others, experience when around these superb creatures. However, I believe that if combined, all of those words could be condensed into one word: "horse."

We ride to fly, to feel, to touch, to laugh, to soar, to overcome, to relax, to heal, to love, and to communicate without words.

We ride to live!

Author Unknown

CHAPTER NINE
Miniature Therapists

On a gorgeous autumn day in October, 2012, granddaughter Katrina (Katie) Dyce, and I drove to Oracle, Arizona, to check out "Little Hooves and Big Hearts" (hereafter referred to as LHBH), the home of miniature therapy horses.

Oracle, a small, rustic mountain town, dates back to 1880, when it was a mining town. Today, it has a population around three thousand six hundred, and is thirty-eight miles north-northeast from downtown Tucson. Its elevation of four thousand feet above sea level— Tucson sits at two thousand five hundred— means its much cooler; often getting snow in the winter, and providing a respite from the heat of summer.

After a short drive through its busy downtown, we wound our way to the ranch. Its high location commands a breathtaking view of the surrounding area.

We were greeted by best friends Tammy Mockbee and Amy Armour. These attractive, kind women are two of the friendliest people I've ever met. Their personalities mirror their little therapists, and it's obvious they love what they do. Their close friendship — they often finish each other's sentences — provided a comfortable, easy atmosphere for Katie and me to learn about the minis.

Tammy Mockbee, LHBH's co-founder along with Patty Green, is an executive director and lead equine therapist, says she "feels blessed to be able to combine her love of horses with her lifelong commitment to helping others." Tammy started riding when she was only four, and she's been around horses ever since. Immediately prior to teaming up with Patty Green to form LHBH, Tammy was a riding instructor, trained horses, and taught equestrian classes.

Tammy has developed an extraordinarily intuitive bond with her equine friends, and she's trained LHBH's ten miniature horses to be highly effective therapy animals.

Her interest in helping people with special needs goes back almost as far as her riding. As an eighth grader in Tucson, she volunteered to work with mentally and physically handicapped kids. Tammy continued her volunteering in high school, helping out at the local senior center, caring for a young boy with epilepsy and spending weekends with a physically disabled couple. In the years since then, she has assisted the Marana School District with its special-needs students and has helped provide home-care services to the elderly. Her gift of empathy now finds full expression at LHBH.

Amy Armour is LHBH's assistant director and one of its equine therapists. Amy has been working with horses and their riders for over twenty-five years. She started out providing house-sitting and animal care services for clients throughout the Tucson area, and later worked as a wrangler and children's counselor at the Tanque Verde Guest Ranch. In 1995, Amy joined the staff of Miraval, where she co-developed and implemented a successful riding program, had various supervisory and managerial responsibilities, and was involved in all of the activities and courses offered by the resort's Trail Department, including the Equine Experience Program that provided instruction in equine therapy. It was at Miraval that Amy met Tammy Mockbee, and in 2010 Amy joined LHBH.

At LHBH Amy assists in evaluating the needs of each client and designing therapy programs that best meet those needs. She also functions as stable manager and shares responsibility for the training, conditioning and care of LHBH's horses.

They describe themselves as facilitators between horses and people — they know the horses and use intuition to read people — which assist people to help themselves. Horses respond to people's energy and told us: horses do not judge; they live in the moment; they have nothing to gain; there is no yesterday, no tomorrow, just now.

They explained that horses are attuned to people. One of their horses, Savannah, can pick out a troubled teen instantly. When she does, her demeanor becomes mellow.

The "minis" go to schools, hospitals, the Children's Diamond Center at the University of Arizona's Medical Center (and hope to go to Tucson Medical Center soon), Girl Scouts at the YMCA Camps, Arizona Foundation for the Handicapped in Casa Grande, anywhere there are children with disabilities, and senior care homes.

The many stories Tammy and Amy relate about the work the horses do are poignant. The one that will always remain with me concerns a gentleman they came across in a senior care facility. They gave me permission to relay it to you:

The man lay tightly curled in a fetal position, eyes firmly shut, close to death. It was felt that he would pass that evening

The horse went into the room, stood close to the bedside, and after a while, appeared to be in a trance state. Slowly, the man's body relaxed; a look of peace softened his face; man and horse were in silent communication. As Tammy put it, "they were in the presence of the angels."

And, as they witnessed peace alter the gentleman's features, this tender scene brought tears to the caregivers who loved him.

Those who know horses are aware of the cord that binds both of their hearts together.

After listening to Amy and Tammy talk about these awe-inspiring creatures, Katie and I couldn't wait to get to meet them. Five of them were expecting us to join them in an outside arena and after mixing and mingling with the group, we were able to choose one apiece, so we could learn how to groom them. I chose the one known as "Grandma;" it seemed fitting. Katie chose Daisy.

I was using my wheelchair that day, but that didn't seem to bother Grandma who kept pace with me as I rolled along, heading for the grooming area. I held the lead rope in my right hand; her head was close to my right shoulder. I'm unsure why I was so overcome by my emotions then. Maybe it was because her closeness gave me comfort. I felt serene and exhilarated at the same time; as if I was with my best friend. Once again, I realized that the more time I spend with a horse, big or small, the more I'm at peace.

Katie has inherited her love of horses from her mother, Kelly, so she was very comfortable with all the horses and we both had a wonderful time grooming them. Katie and I don't have a chance to spend much time together, so I was happy to be able to share that day with her. She's a terrific companion; has a quick wit and fantastic sense of humor.

Only two things marred that day: (1) we couldn't take either of the little guys home with us, and (2) the photos I took that day were lost in an inadvertent mass delete of my camera memory card. The most precious of which was Katie, her long, blonde hair flowing, eyes closed, while cheek-to-cheek she hugged her little treasure, after she'd finished grooming her.

To put them in perspective, their size is designated by the American Miniature Horse Association (AMHA), as less than thirty-four inches at the withers (the ridge between the shoulder blades); while The American Miniature Horse Registry (AMHR) cites "A" Division as thirty-four inches and under, or "B" Division, as thirty-four to thirty-eight inches. All minis are measured at the last hair of the mane (also referred to as withers) and have various colors and coat patterns. The horses at LHBH are registered with both the AMHA and AMHR.

Originally, they were bred as pets for Europe's nobility, but they eventually served other purposes. As they are easy to train and handle and can pull up to three times their body weight, they were worked in mines as "pit ponies."

To retain horse characteristics in a mini-size, miniature horses were developed from multiple sources. Most commonly, Shetlands and Dartmoor ponies were bred with selected smaller, full-size horses.

They retain a horse gene, which ponies do not. They're not, as many assume, ponies. They live longer than some of the full-size breeds, and average a life span from thirty to forty years.

LHBH has eleven horses in their herd, ranging in age from five to eighteen, and from thirty-one and a quarter to thirty-eight inches in height.

Often, when people are unable to go to LHBH's facilities in Oracle, they take the minis to those seniors who reside in nursing homes, assisted living centers, and hospices.

On one of Tucson's special, blue sky, air-smelling-like-freshly-laundered-sheets-waving-from- a-clothes-line Spring days in April, 2013, Doug and I were privileged to accompany Tammy and Amy on a visit to one of the many assisted living centers located in and around Tucson.

We met them in the parking lot area and watched while they prepared Lillie age six, and Dolly, age seven, for their visit. Each horse stood calmly as they were fitted with special booties — Lillie wearing Tartan plaid, Dolly sporting sparkling pink — which protects the flooring as well as their tiny hooves. Special diapers were attached under their tails and after a brushing they were ready to greet the thirty or so residents, and their relatives, who had gathered in the lobby. Smiles and "ohhs" greeted these little wonders.

Tammy and Amy slowly led each of their charges around the circle of residents, and their relatives, stopping in front of them, asking their names, pausing if the person reached toward the composed horse that was used to the role it played as it brought happiness. Some shyly reached forward to touch them; others just watched, seemingly lost in thought; a few slept. Those who made contact always smiled, eliciting broad smiles from their relatives, delighted in the connection that had been made.

One of the residents sat quietly, eyes closed, a doll dressed in a blue and white striped jumper clasped in her left arm. Her great-grandson, Noah, age seven, sat on her right; her great-granddaughter, Katie Funk, age twelve, stood behind her. Lillie stretched her head toward Noah, but stopped as his great-grandmother reached forward to pet her with her right hand; her left arm still firmly gripping the doll.

I had an opportunity to speak with Katie for a bit. Turns out she's been riding horses since she was six — currently at Sabino Equestrian Center — and right now, her goal is to ride in the World Championship Saddlebred competition held annually in Kentucky. She's competed in four states surrounding Arizona, and is constantly working to increase her riding skills.

According to the American Saddlebred Horse Association, "the American Saddlebred is best known for being the ultimate show horse, high stepping and elegant, as he performs his five gaits – the walk, trot, canter, slow gait and rack. The slow gait and rack were developed from the easy-riding gait traits the Saddlebred had inherited. The footfalls of the slow gait and rack begin with the lateral front and hind feet starting almost together, but the hind foot contacts the ground slightly before its lateral forefoot.

The slow gait is a highly-collected gait with each of the four feet striking the ground separately. It is executed slowly but with distinct precision, full of style and brilliant restraint. In the rack, each foot meets the ground at equal, separate intervals. It gives a smooth ride while the horse performs in a slightly uninhibited manner, with great animation, speed and correct form."

The sparkle in Katie's eyes when she spoke about entering the competition along with the determination in her voice makes me believe she'll attain her goal. The word "mirror" is used repetitively by people who work with horses. I'm becoming more aware of it when I'm around the horses, and I wonder what they're reflecting about me.

Often surprising, and touching, mirroring became evident when Tammy escorted Lillie to a lady named Lois, who was sitting to my right. When the horses were first brought around the circle Lois had little or no reaction.

On the second tour of the room, Lillie stopped in front of Lois, looked at her for a bit, and then began to cough. From past experience with Lillie, Tammy knew that this was Lillie's way of indicating that the human she was communicating with wanted water, and asked for someone to bring Lois a glass of water. Then, Lillie began to display chewing movements. (Tammy told me later that this mirrored the energy occurring between horse and the woman).

While still gazing into Lois' eyes, Lillie gently pushed her nose into her right hand. As far as I was able to tell from my angle of sight, there was no visible reaction from her. Then, for a few moments, this tiny marvel tenderly laid her head onto Lois's chest before placing her nose under her chin. Tammy, who'd been kneeling in front of Lois, later told me that at that point, Lillie had entered, and spent time, in Lois's world.

Those sitting across from us reacted by smiling, and saying things like, "Oh," and, "Oh, my." Lois's daughter, who was sitting to her right, began to cry. So did I. But, a few days later, as I looked through the photos I'd snapped that day, I saw the reason why Lois's daughter had cried. At the time, my tears were brought about by the tenderness Lillie had shown to Lois, but Lois's daughter had seen what I wasn't able to.

Even though the photo shows only a portion of the smile that lit up her mother's face, it's enough to reflect the positive energy that had united a bitty wonder horse and wonderful woman.

According to the Capitol Media Services, "On Friday, April 5, 2013, Arizona's Governor, Jan Brewer, signed legislation updating existing laws that cover service animals, meaning that miniature horses (defined as "anything up to thirty-six inches at the shoulder and one hundred pounds) are now included. Up to then, Arizona law did not define what constituted a service animal.

Horses have been included partly because that's what's required by Federal law, and because they are stronger and more able to pull wheelchairs. However, the new law also says individuals can no longer declare they need an animal solely for "comfort" or emotional support. Instead, there is a list of the kinds of work or tasks considered acceptable. These range from helping those with vision or hearing impairment, to pulling wheelchairs, retrieving items and alerting individuals to the presence of allergens.

The federal law, which still must be obeyed, says when a disability is not obvious a business owner may ask only two questions: is the animal required because of a disability and, what work is the animal trained to perform.

They cannot inquire about the person's disability or require medical documentation.

The law allows a property owner to deny admission to a service animal if it is a "threat to the health or safety of others" or "poses an undue burden."

Would you like to adopt a mini, become a friend of Little Hooves, or visit the ranch? I encourage you to check out the Contributor's Page at the back of the book for the necessary information.

CHAPTER TEN
Meet Joey's Other Friends and Caregivers

Joey's Hero: Mike Gorczyca

Before I introduce you to a really great guy, I'd like to pass along my observation about horses' legs and hooves: I don't know how in hell they do the jobs they do! I mean, look at them. For the most part, the legs, which outwardly appear to be the skinniest parts of their anatomy, do all of the ambulatory work — walking, running, pulling, climbing, jumping, with or without the weight of a rider— assisted by unbelievably complex hooves, that are generally only large enough to fit onto a good sized salad plate, but seemingly hold everything together. Too simplistic? Yeah, it is. But take a good look at those appendages. At first, don't they look just as I've described?

When I told you the hoof was complex, I hadn't told you about the three bones that are inside the hooves. The longest is the short pastern bone which extends down from the long pastern bone in the leg. The largest bone in the hoof is the pedal or coffin bone, and beneath the junction of the short pastern bone and the coffin bone is the navicular bone. There are ligaments and tendons running down from the leg and attach to the bones inside the foot.

And, when you learn about the diseases that affect their ability to do all I've described and more — at various speeds, from a slow walk to a full-out gallop — you have to do more than admire the ability of these wonderful creatures to move at all!

Initially, Joey had pain from an abscess in his front hoof, and a hematoma in the rear hoof. Generally speaking, hematomas are pockets of blood developing after blood vessels rupture. Bruises occur for a variety of reasons, such as stepping on sharp stones, and can lead to abscesses and infection within the hoof.

Adding to this was a navicular problem (simplistically meaning degenerative changes in the navicular bone), as well as "high ringbone" (a bone growth which can encircle the bones, thus the name, occurring on the lower part of the large pastern bone or the upper part of the coffin bone) and "low ringbone" (occurring on the lower part of the small pastern bone or the upper part of the coffin bone).

Joey's immune system was poor, so he wasn't fighting off the infection. The infection would come out of the sole (underside of the hoof), or the coronary band (this band runs around the very top of the hoof; similar to our fingernail cuticle).

So the next time your feet hurt, and you want to slip into an easy chair and remove your shoes to free your feet, think about horses. They can't.

Once you comprehend everything that plagued Joey, please remember that Joey originally arrived from a feed lot in Texas. Deb, Bill and subsequently all who entered his life to help him after that time, knew nothing of what happened to him prior. We can ask how, and why, but we'll never know the answers. What we do know is that *our* Joey, who had to be in tremendous pain more often than not, never once lashed out at a caregiver. Rather, he returned the love he received by paying it forward to others.

His love is his legacy.

***

In 1966, Mike Gorczyca interest in shoeing horses was sparked by an article in *Horseman Magazine*.

Originally from Michigan, this friendly, square-jawed, strong (in stature and character) farrier, taught math and science there during the '70s. While there, he shod horses from 1972 until he moved to Tucson in 1983, where he began shoeing again, working with area veterinarians; did some substitute teaching and worked as a framer in construction.

During his time in Michigan, he'd done some shoeing at racetracks, where the owners' attitudes were, "Just fix my horse so he can run." He estimated that over the years, he's shod between seventy-five thousand to one hundred thousand horses.

His description of a farrier: "We're the first line of defense before calling a vet." That's how he met Deb. Three veterinarians recommended corrective shoeing for Joey, who had a quarter inch wide crack in his front foot, and they all suggested she call Mike to fit him for shoes and pads. Quarter cracks are vertical splits in a hoof wall, most commonly found on the inside of the front hooves, or the outside of the hind hooves. At one time, Joey had four quarter cracks — two in each front hoof.

Mike's first impression of Joey, whom he shod for about ten years, was that he was even-tempered, easy to get along with, always cooperative, not easily spooked — a big, friendly, puppy, who loved people. He was never defensive and always accepted everything that was done for him. Mike always felt that Joey had confidence in him; trusted him; there was a mutual admiration between them.

This was obvious on the day that Mike used a Dremel™ tool to clean out a hematoma on the top of the hoof wall on his right hind hoof. Prior to performing this procedure, Mike had gone to the veterinarian's office to view the x-rays of the hoof in order to determine exactly what he'd be dealing with. He saw what looked to be an air pocket — which is how abscesses generally look on x-rays. In fact, it turned out to be a dried hematoma, about the size of a thumbnail, which popped right out. However, after the area was cleaned thoroughly, it left a hole one inch wide and three inches deep that Deb treated with a dried black walnut compound.

Deb said Joey stood quietly during this painful procedure, only moving slightly when the heat from the drilling tool made him uncomfortable, not to get away from Mike.

Wanting to learn about what the process of shoeing entails, on a warm, almost-summer day in May of 2012, Doug and I went to the ranch to watch Mike, along with Robert Burkett whose been assisting him for the past two years, shoe the horses at Wood Haven. When we arrived, Champ, Mama, Dottie, Sapphire and Annie were in their stalls in the barn waiting for their new shoes. Sis wears no shoes, is always barefooted, so her hooves only need to be trimmed.

Deb brought Champ out first, kissed him on the nose, then snapped a clip to either side of his halter. The clips were attached to relatively light chains and are used to cross tie the horse to hold its head still. Champ remained calm throughout what I'd call an ordeal. If someone took an awl and a hammer to my feet, I'd raise a fuss, but no, these magnificent beings take it in stride, and I'm assured there is no pain connected with it, as the nails are placed into the hoof wall which does not have nerves and blood vessels.

Robert, who you'll learn more about in a bit, began the procedure on Champ, while Rocko, short for Rock Star, and one of the other Dalmations wandered in and around the area waiting for their treat — which is the slough from the frog and sole that is pared out of the hoof with a hoof knife after the shoe is removed. Deb says it's full of protein, and must be quite scrumptious, as the dogs ate every bit, and looked for more. Shoeing day must be like Christmas to them.

Mike told me there are approximately a hundred farriers in the Greater Tucson-Sonoita area. The Sonoita area sprawls near the Mexican border in Santa Cruz County, which encompasses the little towns of Elgin, Patagonia, Nogales, Amado, Rio Rico, Tubac, Tumacacori, and a couple of ghost towns.

That area is very picturesque, and contains, among other things, vineyards, Lake Patagonia, and Parker Canyon Lake. And, oh yes, it's horse country.

Both Mike and Robert gave me insights into their work. First of all, there's a bit of danger attached, in the form of bites on your head and shoulders, being kicked, or having your feet stepped on, not to mention (but I will) being peed and shat on. And, when you shoe miniature horses, you have to lay on the ground, so the chances of your being a target for all of that increases. A necessary, but not a glamorous job at all.

As I watched Robert bending over, holding Champ's front hoof, I wondered if bad backs went along with the job, but didn't ask the question. I thought the answer might be obvious; however, Mike considers himself lucky as he only has minor arthritis issues with his back.

Now, Champ's a pretty big guy, standing fifteen point three hands high (from toe to withers); Dottie's at fifteen point two; Annie and Sapphire are at fifteen even; Mama is fourteen point two and Sis is thirty-nine inches.

The Romans were the first to use this measure for horses although some say the Ancient Egyptians were the first. Either way, quite simply, a "hand" is equal to four inches, approximately the width of an adult male's hand, using the fingers only. However, partial hand widths are expressed in inches (nothing is ever easy), so Champ's height of fifteen point three means he's three inches over fifteen hands, as the number three after the decimal is inches, and not a fraction (okay, that's easy).

For an accurate measurement of the height of a horse, it should be standing on firm level ground with its front feet even, or close to even. Using a tape measure placed on the ground, start at the bottom of the outside of the hoof, then take it to the highest point of its withers. When you have ascertained the inches, you'll have to divide that number by four (a hand) and any remainder is the inches above the hand measurement (okay, it's back to not being easy). But a horse who is fifteen point four is actually sixteen point zero hands. Got it? Sure you do. There are special measuring tapes marked in inches and hands — that's the one I'd use.

Before I knew it, Champ was finished, Dottie was up next and Mike took over. She was alternately either bored or bothered by the procedure that he implemented. When he used the grinder on the shoes, which is done to make the shoe balanced and even, it threw sparks. That bothered her.

Mike answered a lot of questions about the reason for the shoeing process and explained, among other things, that the three reasons for shoeing a horse are:

> 1. Protection from excessive wear, which could result in sore hooves, and from small stones/punctures, wounds or bruising;
> 2. Correction of faulty gaits, limb interference and healing of problems such as laminitis and navicular syndrome;
> 3. Traction for high level performance horses (racing, jumping).

I wondered if hooves changed their size with age, and was told that in wet weather the shoes slide back, and the size of the hooves' can change about one size from dry season to wet season. Incidentally, shoeing should be done every six to eight weeks, because the hooves grow, nails rust, and the shoes wear.

Mike's approach to shoeing is to "balance the hooves in pairs" – trims and balances both front hooves, then does the same to the hind hooves.

By balance, he's referring to: (a) toe length, (b) hoof angle, and (c) medial-lateral balance (level at the heels). As with most specialties, there are steps to be followed:

1. Cut clinches (nails)
2. Pull shoes
3. Trim and balance both fronts
4. Trim and balance both hinds
5. Shape and fit shoes
6. Nail shoes on
7. Clinch the nails (bending the nails over using a clinching tool; Mike says it's like tying the laces of a shoe) and finish by rasping hooves and clinches smooth. The number of nails is maybe six or eight, depending on the size of the horse.

Horse shoe nails are uniquely shaped. One side is flat and may contain a pattern or a brand name, the other sided is beveled. The patterned side faces to the inside of the hoof. They're made that way so that when you pound them in, they won't go into the sensitive hoof wall.

Fitting the shoe (balancing) properly is a matter of knowing the horse, reading the foot so you'll know where to place the shoe on the anvil (widen here, narrow there), then fit the shoe to the hoof, eyeball the result and either return to the anvil to make minor adjustments, or start nailing. Mike's been said to be "horsey," meaning he's been around horses long enough (been doing this for forty-two years), that he knows how to get along with them; he knows his profession.

Slippers, such as Joey wore, are similar to "Easy Boots" and fit over the hooves. They're easy to get off and put on; they hold the foam pads close to the sole of the foot. It's like an insole in our shoes.

And now for some information about Mike's assistant, Robert, who began shoeing a few years ago. Prior to that, he'd been a painter, but a few years back, when there was a turndown in the economy, he apprenticed with Mike, began shoeing the horses that his wife, Betsy, owns and now shoes on his own.

Betsy owns and runs the Sarabande Academy of Riding and all information about the Academy is listed on the Contributor's page.

For all of its growth, Tucson is still very much a horse town, but definitely not a "one horse town."

Robert told us that a restaurant on River Road installed a hitching post so people can ride their horses to the restaurant, park their horses, and have a marvelous dinner.

CHAPTER ELEVEN
Dr. Gordon Merayo, DVM.

Dr. Merayo treated Joey for three years before leaving Arizona to open a practice in New Mexico. These are his thoughts:

"I was one of the Veterinarians who participated in Joey's healthcare [treating him for laminitis, and chronic abscesses,] Joey was such a trooper and surprised me more than once on his ability to recover from his severe lameness. As a veterinarian, working with animals (especially animals like Joey) is a pleasure.

"A veterinarian can form strong bonds with the patients. Forming this bond also allows veterinarians to form friendships with the owners of the patients.

"As important as the doctor-patient relationship is, the bond formed with the owners is just as strong and many times a lot stronger. I am very impressed by the dedication that some animal owners have for their pets. Deb and Bill Wood exhibited extreme dedication to Joey. I am grateful for the experience I had to get to know Joey and all of his family."

CHAPTER TWELVE
Amanda Yanez – Equine Body Worker

I met this sweet, attractive, young and slender woman on a gorgeous spring day in March of 2013, at Wood Haven. Amanda was there to work on Annie, who has arthritic hips. When she walked into the barn, Annie immediately came to the front of the stall and greeted her. The bond between them was easy to see. I understand that she's very much loved by all of the horses she works on. Sapphire also has arthritic shoulders; Mama is very sensitive, so touching her should be done with a light touch — she doesn't appreciate being stretched.

There's an ease between those who love and work with horses that I envy. Yes, most animal lovers have a bond, but when that animal is as large as a horse, to be free and easy around them is, to me, something very special. The more I'm around them, the more I feel at ease. Yes, the horses have changed me.

Amanda had always wanted to be a veterinarian. She attended the University of Arizona, where she earned a Bachelor's Degree in Equine Science as working with horses was something she'd always wanted to do. After that, she went on to study Equinology (equine body work) in California, as she thought it looked like something that would help horses.

As she worked on Annie, beginning at the shoulder and neck area on her left side, she talked about Joey, who was her favorite at the time — now, it's Annie. She began working on him over four years ago, and described him as a sweet, curious, gentle soul with kind eyes, who was trusting, never aggressive, and whose favorite spots for massage were his hips, butt, and back flank area. While she worked on him, he'd drop his head down, as if he were going to go to sleep. She knew he'd never bite.

Because of the pain in his hooves, he couldn't stand for prolonged periods of time, and to take the weight off of his hips, she'd work on him while he'd lie down. He was the only horse she'd ever worked on while in that position. She wasn't able to do any leg stretches on him or work near his feet because of how painful that would be.

Amanda did something then that astounded me. Picking up Annie's left front leg, she bent it at the knee then extended it backward, stretching it. Annie didn't seem to mind.

If you've ever had a massage, you know that many who receive them go through a repertoire of noises — grunts, groans, moans — to show either pleasure or, in some instances, pain.

Horses, on the other hand, have a diverse assortment of ways to express their feelings about body work, ranging from licking, chewing, head-rolling, tongue hanging — which show comfort — to farting, peeing, and pooping — indicating a relaxed state. Annie did all of those things.

As Amanda continued the "hold and release" pressure procedure, moving her hands to Annie's underbelly, Annie made chewing movements, and then hung her head. She was *very* relaxed. She also likes to have her teats massaged.

Two years ago, a rattler bit Annie. Immediately after this event, in order to remove the toxins that remained, Amanda guided Deb as she massaged the lymph glands which moved the poison through the lymphatic system to the teats which were then "milked," insuring that the venom was out of her system.

Before Amanda went to the next spot to be worked, she'd test to see if it was sensitive by placing her hand where she intended to work. This also signaled to Annie where Amanda was going next.

As Amanda worked her hands in the hip area, the hip "popped." I asked about the sound and was told that it was normal due to Annie's arthritis and age. Her hands continued to move methodically, testing for muscle tension, and if she found it, she'd work on them individually. The focus is on those areas where the muscles attach to the bones – all two hundred five of them. Unbelievably, one less than the two hundred six we humans possess. For some reason, I thought there'd be more, and when I mentioned this to Amanda, she told me to picture a horse standing on its hind legs. I did that and clearly saw its skeletal structure. Now, you try it. See?

After stretching the hind left leg forward, Amanda picked up Annie's tail, leaned backwards, rotated the tail in circles to relax the muscles, then she pulled it. Annie's tongue came out — obviously, she loved this.

As you might expect, massages "move" things around, causing horses to become thirsty, so at this point in time Annie stopped to take a large drink of water. As she moved into the sun, her coat gleamed, cinnamon gold.

Continuing onto Annie's right side, Amanda did everything she'd done on the left, including stretching both legs. Everything seemed to be in fine order. When she reached the head area, she removed the fly mask to check the TMJ muscles. Annie's head rocked from side to side when Amanda touched the area right behind her ears to check the TMJ muscle.

The temporomandibular joint (TMJ) is critical for a horse's survival and well-being. It has two primary functions, the grinding of food and balance, i.e. its relationship with the ground or posture.

Carrots were used to bribe Annie to bend her neck downward, or turn it to the right or left so that Amanda could work on any of these areas that might require it.

The whole procedure took about an hour. Clearly, Annie enjoyed it, and I enjoyed meeting this truly marvelous woman who provides relief from the aches and pains these magnificent beings sometimes suffer.

CHAPTER THIRTEEN
Meet René Noriega

I've met many fascinating people in connection with the writing of this book; René definitely fits that description, quite possibly for the reason that his life has been so diversified.

In 1979, he enlisted in the Coast Guard, serving in law enforcement and search and rescue teams, but the most intriguing part of that career was serving one year of isolated duty with twenty-seven other "Coasties" on the island of Iwo Jima.

After his enlistment expired, he joined the Douglas, Arizona Police Department, serving three years as both a patrol officer and an investigator, before joining the U. S. Border Patrol in 1988, where he spent twenty-three years working in some of the most remote, lawless parts of this country. There he honed his skills in tracking and "cutting sign," to apprehend drug and people smugglers. More on this a bit later.

For now, we'll chat about René's current expertise which lies in being a Sports Therapist, including the art of Equine Body Work. I'm going to arbitrarily add Bovine as well, as he also works with bulls.

Wanting something to fall back on after he left the Border Patrol, and not being interested in becoming a farrier or a trainer, he looked at Equine Physical Therapy. René went to school, including Michigan State University, one of the only universities offering animal dissection, a class which he took to learn about muscular structure. Eventually, he developed his own way of providing therapy.

René — who's been around horses from the time he could walk — owned his own Egyptian/Arabian horse name Kaileen, and helped his family move cattle — knows what he's talking about.

When he worked with Joey, he said he was able to only make him feel good for a while. Due to the neurological problems Joey suffered, the neuro-response wasn't there. René surmised that those problems may have originated from a fall or other injury.

René's work causes him to be around animals that are in pain. He told me that when an animal's in pain, it creates anxiety which can trigger a "flight or fight" response; the horse becomes defensive. When he's in an arena around rodeo broncs, he keeps his feelings neutral. *Remember what we've learned about horses' reading emotions?* He's been bitten, but never kicked.

However, in Joey's case, "fight or flight" was never an option. René said Joey never complained —

no matter whether he was having a good or bad day. He "ruled." He had "command presence," meaning he understood his role and his place, yet René felt he was a leader to the other horses; they respected him. When horses are ill, it's herd instinct to either surround them for protection or pick on them. Not so with the horses of Wood Haven, they understood Joey's pain and gave him the room he needed to move around.

René told me that animals that are preyed upon will not let anyone know they are hurt until they reach a maximum pain threshold. Massage helps them to "realign" their bodies. René seeks overall "body balance," from the feet to the teeth.

As you would expect someone who works on horses and bulls to be, René is a powerfully built man. Part of his ability to work with horses is his belief that you should "listen" to the horse. There's symmetry in the way their feet hit the ground, so he closes his eyes and listens. What he hears assists him in knowing where the horse is having problems. He uses the same stretch exercises that are used on humans.

He truly respected Joey, saying, "I'll never forget him. Horses such as Joey are few and far between; it's a number greater than one in a million. He had a great spirit, the 'Spirit of Equus," and a bond with people that I've never seen before — he had the gift."

Joey taught René to trust.

Now, I said I'd tell you about René's work with Border Patrol, and I will, I promise. But for just a moment, I'm going off subject.

René knows that having a bond with horses is one thing, among others, that you can never have with bulls. "You can have mutual respect with a bull, but they will jump you in a heartbeat." That's why when he uses therapy on them, he stands outside of their pen and reaches through the bars to perform their body work.

Wonder why we're on this subject? When I interviewed him about Joey, bulls came up in the conversation, so I'm going to digress just a bit and cover this aspect of the exciting life René lives.

One of the reasons I may find it so absorbing is because bull riding is my favorite rodeo event; always has been. I think they're intriguing animals.

René's cousin raises these enormous creatures for bull riding competition, which affords him the opportunity to be around them; a lot. "Cowboy" is René's personal bull; he's huge, white in color, and truly impressive. In 2011, Cowboy's brother was National Champion, bringing in close to a million dollars.

A year ago in March, his cousin gave him a bull that had been "bullied" by other bulls, and he took him to Elfrida, Arizona for rehab. By June, he was able to bring him from one thousand pounds to one thousand six hundred fifty pounds. I believe you'll find a photo of him on René's website (see Contributor's Page) and he's the reason I added bovine body work along with equine body work.

By the way, he's also massaged the pack mules at the Grand Canyon. Pretty cool, huh?

Now, back to the Border Patrol. René worked the Tucson Sector, which encompasses the area between the New Mexico border and the Yuma County, Arizona line, including the Air Force bombing range outside of Yuma. As I previously mentioned, some of this country is rugged and remote, and using four-wheeled vehicles to track people or drug smugglers isn't the most expeditious means of transportation.

René: "When you're tracking somebody, you need to become the aggressor."

Horses can go where vehicles can't, so in 1997, while in the Nogales, Arizona Border Patrol Station on the U.S./Mexico Border, he instituted the Border Patrol Horse Patrol in Arizona. Because he grew up in southeastern Arizona around horses, he was able to combine those two facets to enhance his ability to track and cover terrain expeditiously and efficiently.

Eventually, René developed a training program with an operational application where an agent could attend and be certified to perform the functions of a "mounted agent" who would have the ability to track/cut sign and move in terrain that was not easily accessed by other means of transportation.

Initially, the Patrol members used their personal horses. As Patrol members saw how effective horses were in this effort, René went to his boss and said, "We need money for horses." The answer? "We don't have money for that, so catch what you can."

The horses they "caught" were horses that were indigenous to the area. That's a nice way of saying that they'd been used to carry drug loads into the U.S. They'd been badly mistreated; used and abused; left to wander, and to die. They were malnourished, worn out; beat up.

The loads, more often than not, are so heavy the horses are unable to carry them far. When the loads are cut off, the horses are left to wander, but sometimes are returned across the border where their hell begins again.

Back then, when the horses were found, they were so afraid they wouldn't let anyone touch them. It took six months to a year to return them to health. A maintenance program was developed — vet care, hoof care, nutrition. If they were able, they were put into Border Patrol service. When they were through, they were often adopted by the agents they'd been assigned to; if not they were given to the state to auction off.

Initially, there were three; now there are one hundred and forty.

That was then. Now, when horses are found, they're turned over to the state to be auctioned off, or otherwise placed. There are many horse rescue ranches in the Tucson area; there are always more horses than there are places for them. There have been many television documentaries done on the plight of these horses; the rescue ranches are always in need of funds. If you're interested, an Internet search could help you to find them in your area.

René was also instrumental in developing the SEMOTT School. Strategic Equine Mobile Operations – SEMO is the process of moving people and resources in a stealthy and covert manner across rugged terrain that is generally inaccessible by vehicles or aircraft;

TT is the application of trailing, tracking, stalking, and sign cutting in determining the intent and operational schemes by detecting, deducting, and identifying environmental disturbance caused by humans.

The tracking is done using the Apache method of tracking, also known as cutting sign. Anything that moves leaves tracks or signs: a broken twig, a leaf that shouldn't be in the area; an overturned rock; the form of a footprint will tell you whether the human was running, walking fast, carrying a heavy load, etc. Being observant is paramount.

Many of the techniques in this program have been adopted and implemented by the Border Patrol, and this program has been taught to the FBI, Homeland Security, and various Sheriff's Departments in Border States.

As I told you initially, he leads a diversified and fascinating life.

CHAPTER FOURTEEN
To The Beat Of A Drum. . .

You've read the back stories of the horses of Wood Haven. Have you wondered, or doubted their validity? Are you one who accepts things you're told without questioning, or do you try to keep an open mind, despite raising an eyebrow? Either way, I'll set down the facts, and let you decide.

In the beginning, I freely admit to a skosh of skepticism, but the sincerity and honesty imparted by Deb, and others, during the relating of their accounts not only kept my mind open, but made me keen to experience the ability to do what they had done: communicate with animals. I can hear it now, "Yeah, you and Dr. Dolittle." Okay, I'll give you that. But, hear me out.

When I asked Deb how she came to be able to communicate with her horses, she told me about Linda Johns, communicator, healing practitioner and founder of Journey to Healing.

Initially, I spoke with Linda twice by phone. Between that and the information contained on her website, I found out that Linda has many years of training, study and experience in both the healing arts and in spiritual studies, and holds certifications from the Institute of Health and Healing, the International

Breath Institute and the Wildfire Holistic Animal Healing Center, as well as being certified as a Reiki Master/Teacher, an animal communicator, a spiritual path finder and she has reached the level of master studies in the Inner Wisdom Mystery School. She has also studied with a medicine woman in healing traditions.

She's a strong woman, who told me during one of our chats, "I don't have to prove myself to anyone" and, she doesn't. She's got a track record of working with veterinarians, and others, both locally and long-distance in other states and countries where these healing techniques are practiced and greatly appreciated.

A voice for animals, information comes to her from the animal she's working with, sometimes visually, sometimes as a silent voice, and she passes it onto the vet or pet owner, who acts on it accordingly.

Linda's work has been featured in numerous magazines, newspapers, television and radio. She has taught at Pima Community College in Tucson, Arizona, works at the Immune Recovery and Wellness Center, and provides additional private classes at her home.

She lives on a desert ranch near Tucson with her family and two dogs, three cats, three horses, two burros, chickens, Koi, a tortoise and many wild animal visitors, all of whom are willing to help students learn to communicate with them.

It was there, on a beautifully sunny, spring day in May, 2013 that I joined eight other women who wanted to experience and learn how to communicate. I intended that last sentence to end as it did — without adding the words "with animals," simply because one of the first things Linda discussed was "active listening," which applies to humans as well.

"Active listening" means concentrating on what's being said to you without jumping in and finishing the speaker's sentence, or letting your mind wander, or thinking about your answer before the speaker has finished.

But, before going into the depth of the class, Linda crouched before a drum of just the right size: not too big, not too small, but just the right size, and admonished us to take deep breaths, use a simple grounding technique, say any words that would become a prayer of focus and intent, and with eyes closed banish all negative thoughts and moods that might encroach from the outside world.

And to the beat of the drum, that's what we did.

Maybe it was the hypnotic rhythm of the drum beat, maybe it was the light breeze blowing through the window, or maybe it was the communal feeling that was generated by women who share a love for animals and were intent on learning, but whatever it was, for me, gently telling the world to take a hike was liberating. I was at peace, and eager to learn.

With the assistance of Linda's two dogs, and two of her three cats (who for the most part remained in the house with us), and later on, her horses and the burros whom several of us joined outside, the process of learning to communicate began.   Through   a series of exercises, we began the difficult tasks that learning to communicate with animals requires: learning how to banish self-doubt (a lifelong challenge for me); the dare of expanding our world; the letting go of fears and overcoming ego; allowing instincts, telepathy and intuition to develop, along with the ability to discern the difference between our voice and the voice of the animal.

Communication with animals isn't easy, and it certainly can't be done in four hours. However, I did learn techniques that require daily practice with my cats, and experienced communication with Blaze, one of Linda's horses.

After we'd worked on the exercises, we were given a chance to try them out on any of the dogs, cats, or horses of our choice. I chose the horses, so accompanied by Deb (who'd been invited as a guest, and who'd brought her childhood friend, Kim, from Ohio, with her) we walked out to the corrals, where I spotted a twenty-one year old black Mustang, named Blaze. As I approached him, I remembered that Deb's horse, Champ, doesn't like my cane, and I worried that it might spook him, too, so I hung it on a tree branch, and Deb walked me to the corral, where I stood in front of him. I closed my eyes.

For the life of me, I couldn't remember his name, but following Linda's instructions, attempted bridging between me and him by calling him "no name" three times, telling him my name, and asking if he'd like to speak to me. No answer.

Then, I asked him what he liked to do? The words, "Be anywhere but here," popped into my mind. I opened my eyes to see Blaze moving from where I stood into the corral next to where he'd been standing. I laughed, and told Deb what I'd heard, then commented that since he'd moved away, I guessed that it meant that he didn't want to be standing near me. *Lesson*: remove your ego. I'd forgotten that.

Blaze wandered to another of the women, so I stood at the corral fence looking towards the burros, and tried to call one of them over using telepathy, but that didn't work. Instead, Blaze came up to me and began to nibble on my fingers. I apologized for not having treats, but he continued to nibble gently.

Just as Deb and I decided to go back into the house, Blaze reached for my arm and I got the impression that he was going to nibble on the sleeve of my shirt, but by then I'd moved away.

When we joined the circle once again, Linda asked if anyone had had any success. I related my story, and got this answer from Linda:

Blaze was new to the ranch, having arrived six months prior because there'd been a death in the former owner's family, so he'd been "rehomed." He was having a hard time dealing with the other horse, Tug, who was being very assertive. So, when I heard the words, "be anywhere but here," she took it to mean that he wanted to go back to where he'd come from. We believe I had communicated with Blaze!

But, I'd forgotten another of the lessons. When Blaze moved off, instead of laughing at the answer I'd heard, thinking it'd been about my proximity to him (there's that ego thing), I should have kept at it with a follow-up question. It didn't matter that he'd physically moved, I could have continued to maintain the connection with a follow up. Maybe, "where would you like to be?" Or, a simple, "Why?" Hindsight is great, huh? I'll remember that the next time.

Linda also told us that Blaze's former owner had been blind, so he'd taken to placing treats in many places in his clothes, and he and Blaze played a game of "finding the treats," so when Blaze reached for the sleeve of my shirt, he was playing the game with me.

That not only pleased me, it touched my heart. I'd made a connection. Although I met some very special women that day, there was one who stood out to me. Her name is Katelyn Powers, and she runs Spay and Neuter Solutions. This organization does exactly as the name implies. Through advertising and word-of-mouth she performs this service, saving small animals from, well, you know.

By the end of June, 2013, if she can provide the service to one hundred and ninety-nine more animals, she will have saved over ten thousand little lives.

She asks only a small co-pay for this priceless benefit, and often runs specials such as the "Testicle Festival" this past February, and "Sexless in Tucson." Her contact information is on the Contributor's page.

CHAPTER FIFTEEN
Meet Lynn Younger

Over fifteen years ago, a personal health challenge led Lynn Younger from her career as a graphics designer to explore methods of alternative healing. She discovered colorpuncture chromatherapy, a modality of acupuncture and color therapy, a revolution in holistic healing and one of Europe's most popular new alternative healing disciplines.

Deb met Lynn when she became interested in colorpuncture light work, which is the belief that the simple application of color vibrations can achieve remarkable changes in physical, emotional, mental and spiritual body. Light is subtle in effect, fast moving and penetrates deeply into all cells of the body.

It's based on the modern science of photobiology, wherein researchers discovered that light is actually the medium by which cells communicate and it is at the very basis of many body functions. This is true for animal as well as humans.

Lynn lives in another of my favorite Arizona towns— Sedona— and we spoke briefly by phone this past June.

She told me that she'd rather work with animals ('four-legged'), than humans ('two-legged'), saying that "animals' [thoughts] are not cluttered as humans are.

You're not dealing with a 'personality' as you do with a human." This, she felt, was why Joey was successful in his therapy work. The vibration is different between humans and animals.

Much of her work involves communicating with animals. She said that when "When you ask a four-legged a question, they're answer is succinct; in few words. They don't elaborate as humans will."

She telepathically communicated with Joey while Deb (who was holding a cell phone), was in the barn with him. When Lynn asked if he was in pain, the answer came to her in the form of the color red. She then asked him what the level of his pain was, and the answer she received was, "Always."

These answers helped guide Deb to know what color of light to use in order to alleviate the pain. To better understand the benefits of color and its use on physical as well as emotional problems, see Deb's and Lynn's website information on the Contributors page.

When we spoke about animal communication, she also reiterated some of the things I'd learned in my class with Linda Johns: communication is about intuition. Lynn advised writing down what you hear without trying to figure it out; write down what you feel, even if it's wrong.

Lynn felt that although Joey got along with the herd, he was different, elevated, not just a horse. She felt that at one time he may have been two-legged. "He's lived in both worlds, but not at the same time."

You can find out more about Lynn and her work on her website. I believe you'll find it fascinating.

CHAPTER SIXTEEN
Juliana Rose Teal

On Saturday, March 10, 2012, Deb had finished a lecture on the Introduction of Light and Color application at New Moon Haven, in Catalina, Arizona, and was standing at the front counter speaking with the owners about the energy in the room during her lecture, which she described as the most incredible feeling she'd ever experienced.

Knowing that it was so lovingly received, she felt that it was the greatest lecture she'd ever given. The love and compassionate energy from everyone involved made the healing process flow beautifully.

That's when Rose Teal walked in; intense concentration shadowing her face as she approached Deb.

She asked, "Who is the black and white Paint horse standing behind your right shoulder?"

Deb replied, "That's Sir Joey. He passed a little over a year ago."

Juliana began rubbing her leg, "Why is he showing me his leg between the knee and hoof?"

Deb explained," He had high and low ringbone and navicular problems but his feet were the most visible areas of discomfort."

Julianna continued, "He wants you to know that his legs now have a tickling, tingling feeling."

To Deb, that meant he had no more pain!

"He's showing me a grey horse," Juliana said, "And I'm repeatedly hearing the words 'flea bitten grey.' Do you think that means he's coming back again as a grey horse?"

Deb said, "I think he's telling me that he's found Pepper, a barn-mate of his who preceded him due to skin cancer."

"Now," Juliana continued, "he's showing me a white horse. Are you purchasing a white horse?"

Deb told her, "No."

Juliana said, "I'm definitely seeing a white horse."

Neither woman could figure that one out – then.

"Well, he also wants you to know that he loves the sign you had made for him," and then described the shape, color, and the words that were written on the sign.

"He must mean the sign I had made for him at a Street Fair several years ago. It has his picture and the name "Joey' on it. He wanted everyone to call him "Joey" because "Joe" was for those with "two legs," and he had four! I have it on a shelf next to his fly mask in the living room of the barn."

Prior to that conversation, Juliana only knew Deb did equine therapy — Deb knew that Juliana was an astrologer. Matter of fact, her husband Bill had Juliana do a reading for him. Joey's existence had never been mentioned to her, and she'd never visited their barn.

Juliana Rose Teal, astrologer, intuitive, medium, pilot, is pretty and bright; whose warm, friendly smile would make butterflies dance, instantly makes you want her for a friend. But, it's her eyes that are unforgettable and draw her to you. Light blue in color, circled by a dark blue ring, they home in on your heart — in a good way.

Although she'd been aware of her psychic and intuitive gifts all of her life, she suppressed them until her mid-twenties when they became intense and, as she put it, "the gates opened."

One day, she had a vision of buildings burning, then falling; people running and screaming. The visualization was so vivid she became frightened, and cowered, trembling in her room. She didn't understand what she'd seen until three days later, on April 19, 1995, when the Alfred P. Murrah Federal Building was destroyed. She realized then that she'd seen the Oklahoma City bombing, and could no longer deny her spirituality.

In 1991, she attended the University of Washington, receiving a degree in Psychology in 1998.

It was at that time that her interest in the metaphysical took hold. She began studying astrology, and other cultures, began to give readings (initially free for two years), but after those two years, when someone paid her for a reading, she realized that "this is what I'm supposed to do." Her path having been shown to her, in her words, she "never looked back."

In 2002, she moved to Tucson from Seattle, and while working on charts began to have visions and soon realized she was a medium. She says the visions can't be forced; they come to her unbidden.

When she met Deb Wood in 2012, at New Moon Haven in Catalina, and saw the black and white horse standing behind her, the vision was very intense. The communication of a picture of a grey horse, and references to a "flea bitten grey horse," as well as "a white horse," didn't have much meaning at the time either.

However, soon after, Deb was informed by her friend, Julie, that her *grey* horse, Maggie, was in foal, and that all signs pointed to it being male.

Was Joey indicating that he's going to return as a grey? Will the foal be his color, or will the youngster begin to exhibit the same gifts that Joey had? Things will become clearer in May — when the colt is due to be born. Incidentally, since the colt is half-Draft, it might just be a big 'un.

(Photo by Julie Cole Mitchell)

UPDATE: On May 27, 2013, at approximately 10:30 a.m. "Majestic Moment," barn name, Maggie, foaled "A Soldier's Moment," barn name Cadet. His Sire is "Sapphire's Cream of the Crop," who is *white* in color.

Were Joey's references to "flea bitten grey" and "white horse" meant to convey the color of Cadet's parental lineage? You can draw your own conclusions.

But there's one more thing you should know about this remarkable woman: although at one time she had a flying phobia, she now pilots planes and is currently learning how to handle a helicopter!

In 2001, during a flight from Tucson to California, while admiring the blue sky and fluffy white clouds hovering above her plane window, she wondered what it would be like to fly an airplane. And, just that quickly, her phobia left.

When she returned to Tucson, she found a small airport and met a flight instructor who asked her if she'd like to "see a plane." After climbing into the cockpit she fell in love with the plane and knew she had to fly.

Over the next four years she took scenic air rides every few months when she was able to afford them. In 2005, she began flight training in a Cessna 172 four-seat propeller plane (her favorite plane is a Piper Arrow), and in 2007 received her pilot's license. She's trained in instrument flying (used when visibility is nil), and is now learning to handle the controls of a helicopter, which is "ten times harder than flying planes," but her perseverance and discipline is paying off.

Check into her website to watch her fly a helicopter. (See Contributors' Page).

Like I said, she's amazing.

CROSSING THE RAINBOW BRIDGE

The story tells of a green meadow located on our side of the gate to heaven. Rainbow Bridge is the name of both the meadow and an adjoining bridge connecting it to Heaven. Although no major religion specifically endorses such a place for pets, the belief shows similarities with the Bifröst bridge of Norse mythology.

According to the story, when a pet dies, it goes to the meadow, having been restored to perfect health and free of any injuries. The pet runs and plays all day with the others, there is always fresh food and water, and the sun is always shining. However, it is said that while the pet is at peace and happy, they miss their owner who had to be left behind on Earth.

When their owner dies, they come across the Rainbow Bridge. It is at that moment that their pet stops what they are doing, sniffs at the air and looks into the distance where they see their beloved owner. Excited, they run as fast as they can until they are in their owner's arms, licking their face in joy while their owner looks into the eyes of their pet who was absent on Earth, but never absent in their heart. Then side by side, they cross the Rainbow Bridge together into Heaven, never again to be separated.

CONTRIBUTORS'CONTACT INFORMATION

Amanda Yanez — Equine Body Worker —
    email: deserthorse1@hotmail.com

Bill Wood — Wood's Plumbing -13880 N. Adonis
Road, Marana, Arizona, 85658 —
    www.woodsplumbing.com

Deb Wood — Wood Haven Healing Center
    www.WoodhavenHealing.com;
    email: woodhavenhealing@aol.com

Juliana Rose Teal: Astrologer, intuitive, medium
    www.HawkFlightAstrology.com

Katelyn Powers —
    www.spayandneutersolutions.org.
    email:help@SpayandNeuterSolutions.org.

Kelly Hall - Happy Hoof Pads –
    www.HappyHoofPads.com;
    happyhoof@tampabay.rr.com

Little Hooves and Big Hearts — Amy Armour and
Tammy Mockbee—
    email:LittleHooves@me.com
    http://LittleHoovesAndBigHearts.org

Linda Johns —
    email: journeytohealing@msn.com; —
    www.journeytohealing.com

Mary Ann Hutchison —
   www.BloominCane.com
   email:mahutch1936@comcast.net

Rene Noriega —
   www.Equistride.com

The Center of Hope - Dale Hallen –
   www://TheCenterofHopeTucson.com

PENtagram Consulting
   www.PentagramConsulting.net

BOOKS AND MOVIES ABOUT HORSES
(FOR THE YOUNG
AND THE YOUNG AT HEART)

Black Beauty - by Anna Sewell

[The] Black Stallion – by Walter Farley

Misty of Chincoteague – by Marguerite Henry & Wesley Dennis

My Friend Flicka – by Mary O'Hara*

National Velvet – Enid Bagnold*

****

"Buck" – Ifc Independent (Real Life Story)
The Man From Snowy River – 20th Century Fox

Wild Hearts Can't Be Broken – Walt Disney Studios

*Also a movie

Made in the USA
Las Vegas, NV
15 January 2022